LIVES OF GREAT RELIGIOUS BOOKS

The *I Ching*

LIVES OF GREAT RELIGIOUS BOOKS

The *I Ching*

A BIOGRAPHY

Richard J. Smith

PRINCETON UNIVERSITY PRESS

Princeton and Oxford

Copyright © 2012 by Princeton University Press

Published by Princeton University Press, 41 William Street,

Princeton, New Jersey 08540

In the United Kingdom: Princeton University Press, 6 Oxford Street,

Woodstock, Oxfordshire OX20 1TW

press.princeton.edu

Library of Congress Cataloging-in-Publication Data

Smith, Richard J. (Richard Joseph), 1944–

The I Ching : a biography / Richard J. Smith.

p. cm. — (Lives of great religious books)

Includes bibliographical references and index.

ISBN 978-0-691-14509-9 (hardcover : alk. paper)   1. Yi jing.   I. Title.

PL2464.Z7S63 2012

299.5′1282—dc23

2011041070

British Library Cataloging-in-Publication Data is available

This book has been composed in Garamond Premier Pro

Printed on acid-free paper. ∞

Printed in the United States of America

10 9 8 7 6 5 4 3 2 1

For the literary members of my family, Lisa and Tyler,

in celebration of Negative Capability, and with

unbounded admiration, gratitude, and love

Contents

CONTENTS

List of Illustrations

The Hexagrams

Hexagram	Number	Chinese Character	Chinese Name
䷀	1	乾	Qian
䷁	2	坤	Kun
䷂	3	屯	Zhun
䷃	4	蒙	Meng
䷄	5	需	Xu
䷅	6	訟	Song
䷆	7	師	Shi
䷇	8	比	Bi
䷈	9	小畜	Xiaoxu [Xiaochu]
䷉	10	履	Lü

Hexagram	Number	Chinese Character	Chinese Name
䷊	11	泰	Tai
䷋	12	否	Pi
䷌	13	同人	Tongren
䷍	14	大有	Dayou
䷎	15	謙	Qian
䷏	16	豫	Yu
䷐	17	隨	Sui
䷑	18	蠱	Gu
䷒	19	臨	Lin
䷓	20	觀	Guan
䷔	21	噬嗑	Shihe
䷕	22	賁	Bi
䷖	23	剝	Bo
䷗	24	復	Fu

Hexagram	Number	Chinese Character	Chinese Name
䷘	25	无妄	Wuwang
䷙	26	大畜	Daxu [Dachu]
䷚	27	頤	Yi
䷛	28	大過	Daguo
䷜	29	坎	Kan [Xikan]
䷝	30	離	Li
䷞	31	咸	Xian
䷟	32	恆	Heng
䷠	33	遯	Dun
䷡	34	大壯	Dazhuang
䷢	35	晉	Jin
䷣	36	明夷	Mingyi
䷤	37	家人	Jiaren
䷥	38	睽	Kui

Hexagram	Number	Chinese Character	Chinese Name
䷦	39	蹇	Jian
䷧	40	解	Xie
䷨	41	損	Sun
䷩	42	益	Yi
䷪	43	夬	Kuai [Guai]
䷫	44	姤	Gou
䷬	45	萃	Cui
䷭	46	升	Sheng
䷮	47	困	Kun
䷯	48	井	Jing
䷰	49	革	Ge
䷱	50	鼎	Ding
䷲	51	震	Zhen
䷳	52	艮	Gen

THE HEXAGRAMS

Hexagram	Number	Chinese Character	Chinese Name
䷴	53	漸	Jian
䷵	54	歸妹	Guimei
䷶	55	豐	Feng
䷷	56	旅	Lü
䷸	57	巽	Sun [Xun]
䷹	58	兌	Dui
䷺	59	渙	Huan
䷻	60	節	Jie
䷼	61	中孚	Zhongfu
䷽	62	小過	Xiaoguo
䷾	63	既濟	Jiji
䷿	64	未濟	Weiji

Chronology of Chinese Dynasties

Note: Much debate surrounds the dating of the earliest Chinese dynasties (especially the Xia, which many scholars consider to be semihistorical), and even later dates are sometimes highly contested.

Dynastic Name			Chinese Name	Dates
Pinyin	Wade-Giles	Subperiods		
Xia	Hsia		夏	ca. 2000–ca. 1600 BCE
Shang	Shang		商	ca. 1600–ca. 1050 BCE
Zhou	Chou		周	ca. 1050–256 BCE
		Spring and Autumn Period	春秋	ca. 770 BCE–ca. 476 BCE
		Warring States Period	戰國	ca. 475 BCE–221 BCE
Qin	Ch'in		秦	221 BCE–206 BCE
Han	Han		漢	206 BCE–220 CE

| Dynastic Name | | | Chinese | |
Pinyin	Wade-Giles	Subperiods	Name	Dates
Six Dynasties Period			六朝	220–589
Sui	Sui		隋	589–618
Tang	T'ang		唐	618–907
Five Dynasties Period			五代	907–960
Song	Sung		宋	960–1279
Yuan	Yüan		元	1279–1368
Ming	Ming		明	1368–1644
Qing	Ch'ing		清	1644–1912

Preliminary Remarks
and Acknowledgments

The curse of China studies for Westerners has always been the transliteration of Chinese sounds. For many years the scholarly (and popular) convention was to use the so-called Wade-Giles system for rendering Chinese names, terms, and titles, which is why so many people in the West know the *Classic of Changes* as the *I Ching*. I have retained this long-standing usage in the title of this biography, but in the body of the book I have rendered it according to the more current Pinyin system of transliteration: hence, *Yijing*. I have employed similarly standard conventions for the transliteration of other Asian names but have eliminated most diacritical marks and have tried to keep technical terms and titles to a minimum. For instance, although the two characters for *Yijing* are pronounced (and therefore transliterated) in sometimes radically different ways in Japanese (*Ekikyo*), Korean (*Yokkyong*), Vietnamese (*Dich Kinh*), and Tibetan (*Yi Kying*), I have used only the Chinese (Pinyin) transliteration of this title in the text, regardless of the culture area under discussion. In the same spirit, I have translated into English (or used already common renderings of) virtually all the technical words, expressions, terms, and titles in the main part of this book, relegating transliterations to the index, in parentheses that follow the translated terms and titles.

Since this book is designed primarily for nonspecialists, I have not burdened it with detailed descriptions, elaborate footnotes, discussions of arcane scholarly debates, or extensive bibliographies in Asian and Western languages. Material of this sort may be found in my 2008 book, *Fathoming the Cosmos and Ordering the World: The* Yijing *(I-Ching, or Classic of Changes) and Its Evolution in China*. I am grateful to the University of Virginia Press for permitting me to draw from parts of this work in my discussion of the domestic development of the *Changes*. I might add that the acknowledgments, notes, and bibliographies of *Fathoming the Cosmos* reveal abundantly the profound debt I owe to my teachers in the China field, my many valuable friends and colleagues at Rice University, and a host of other scholars around the world, several of whom also deserve special mention here for their specific contributions to this volume: Joseph Adler, Alejandro Chaoul, Howard Goodman, Tze-ki Hon, Pei Jin, Yung Sik Kim, Livia Kohn, Liu Dajun, Richard John Lynn, Naturaleza Moore, Benjamin Wai-ming Ng, Bent Nielsen, Valrae Reynolds, Hyong Rhew, Dennis Schilling, Edward Shaughnessy, Shen Heyong, Kidder Smith, Benjamin Wallacker, Wang Mingxiong, and Zhang Wenzhi.

There are literally hundreds of Western-language translations of the *Yijing* (also known as the *Zhou*

Changes), several of which I discuss in chapter 5. For this biography I have drawn upon, and modified when necessary, five well-known renderings that reflect different understandings of the work as they developed at different periods in Chinese history: (1) Richard Kunst's dissertation, titled "The Original *Yijing*" (1985), which offers a heavily annotated translation of the earliest layers of the so-called basic text (c. 800 BCE); (2) Richard Rutt's *Zhouyi* (1996), which has a similar chronological focus but is less technical and more accessible; (3) Edward Shaughnessy's *I Ching* (1996), which translates a second-century BCE version of the *Changes* that was discovered at Mawangdui (Hunan province) about four decades ago; (4) Richard John Lynn's *The Classic of Changes* (1994), which not only provides a rendering of the work after it became a classic in 136 BCE but also offers a highly influential third-century CE commentary on the *Yijing*, as well as abundant notes on later interpretations of the work; and (5) Richard Wilhelm's *The I Ching or Book of Changes* (1967), based on a Song dynasty (960–1279 CE) understanding of the text that became the orthodox interpretation from the fourteenth century into the early twentieth.

For a reference book on *Yijing* scholarship and technical terminology, there is no better English-language resource than Bent Nielsen's *A Companion to Yi jing Numerology and Cosmology: Chinese Studies of Images and Numbers from Han (202 BCE–220 CE) to Song (960–1279 CE)* (2003), which is organized alphabetically by Pinyin transliterations of names, terms, and titles. Another extremely useful reference work, in German, is Dennis Schilling's *Yijing: Das Buch der Wandlungen* (2009), which attempts to capture the earliest meaning of the *Changes* while also offering valuable information on the complex history of the classic.

The *I Ching*

Introduction

For those who think of themselves as secular, rational, and scientific, the *Yijing* seems to be a work of "awesome obscurity," full of unfamiliar symbols and cryptic sayings, and reflecting a worldview sometimes described as "mystical" or "prelogical." And for those of a more religious disposition, the lack of a cosmology based on the willful actions of a god or gods seems equally puzzling. In either case the *Changes* appears to be little more than a series of briefly annotated broken and solid lines that have no meanings except for those arbitrarily imposed on them by centuries of often-conflicting Chinese commentaries.

Yet there is logic to the work, which, for at least three thousand years, China's greatest minds have sought to fathom and articulate. Into the twentieth century, the *Yijing* occupied a central place in Chinese culture, from the realms of philosophy, religion, art, and literature to those of politics and social life. Thinkers of every intellectual persuasion found inspiration in the language, symbolism, and imagery of the *Changes*. The work also inspired many impressive artistic and literary achievements, and it provided an analytical vocabulary that proved extraordinarily serviceable in virtually every area of elite and popular culture, including science and technology. In premodern times, Chinese scientists used *Yijing*-derived symbolism, numerology, and mathematics to explain a wide range of natural processes and phenomena in the fields of knowledge that we now call physics, astronomy, chemistry, biology, medicine, meteorology, and geology. And even today many devotees of the *Changes* see in the mathematical symbolism of the document the seeds of modern scientific theories, from the binary logic of computers to the structure of DNA. In short, to understand much of Chinese history and culture, we need to understand the *Changes*.

From the Han dynasty (206 BCE–220 CE) through the Qing (1644–1912 CE), the *Yijing* remained a work of enormous and unchallenged scriptural authority; everyone in Chinese society esteemed it and employed it in some way, from emperors and officials to artisans and peasants. Commoners used pages from the book as a charm to ward off evil, and scholars gave it pride of place as "first among the [Confucian] classics." Although the document contains few explicit references to supernatural beings or supernatural forces, it has always had a profoundly spiritual dimension. Indeed, the *Changes* describes itself as "the most spiritual thing in the world." By virtue of its spiritual power, we are told, the *Yijing* "lets one know what is going to come, and by virtue of its wisdom, it becomes a repository of what has happened."[1] But whereas most religious traditions, both East and West, have emphasized the activities of a god or gods as an explanation for cosmic processes, devotees of the *Changes* have long held the view that such explanations reside in the cosmic powers embodied in its lines, trigrams, and hexagrams.

The central preoccupation of the *Yijing* throughout the imperial era (from the Han to the Qing) was how to understand the patterns and processes of nature, and how to act in harmony with them. The most common term for nature in premodern China was Dao, usually translated as "the Way." Although this long-standing metaphysical concept had neither a personality nor a particular identity, it remained an overarching unifying truth among the Chinese in the same general sense that concepts such as Yahweh, Allah, God, Brahman, and Ultimate Reality were in the Judaic, Islamic, Christian, Hindu, and Buddhist traditions, respectively. To fathom the Dao was to understand the various types of change in the universe, from the cosmic to the mundane, from recurrent cycles of movement—ebb and flow, rise and decline, advance and retreat—to physical and metaphysical transformations. From this sort of understanding came an appreciation of proper timing and positioning, essential in a culture where the ritual ideal had always been to do the right thing, at the right time, in the right place, facing the right direction.

What Is the *Yijing* and How Does It Work?

The *Changes* first took shape about three thousand years ago as a divination manual, consisting of sixty-four six-line symbols known as hexagrams. Each hexagram was uniquely constructed, distinguished from all the others by its combination of solid (——) and/or broken (— —) lines. The first two hexagrams in the conventional order are Qian and Kun; the remaining sixty-two hexagrams represent permutations of these two paradigmatic symbols.

Qian   Kun

At some point in the Zhou dynasty (ca. 1045–256 BCE), no later than the ninth or eighth century, each hexagram acquired a name, a brief description known as a "judgment," and a short explanatory text for each of its six lines called a "line statement." This highly compact document, less than 4,200 characters in length and probably first inscribed on strips of bamboo, became known as the basic text of the *Yijing*. The operating assumption of the *Changes*, as it developed over time, was that these hexagrams represented the basic circumstances of change in the universe, and that by selecting a particular hexagram or hexagrams and correctly interpreting the various symbolic elements of each, a person could gain insight into the patterns of cosmic change and devise a strategy for dealing with

4

problems or uncertainties concerning the present and the future.

During the third century BCE, a set of diverse and poetic commentaries known as the "Ten Wings" became attached to the *Changes*, and the work received imperial sanction in 136 BCE as one of the five major Confucian classics. These Ten Wings—particularly the so-called Great Commentary—articulated the *Yijing*'s implicit cosmology and invested the classic with an alluring philosophical flavor and an attractive literary style. The worldview of this amplified version of the *Changes* emphasized correlative thinking, a humane cosmological outlook, and the fundamental unity of Heaven, Earth, and Humanity. For the next two thousand years or so, the *Yijing* held pride of place in China as the first of the Confucian classics.

How does the document work? The first point to be made is that the *Changes* allows, and even encourages, an enormous amount of interpretive flexibility; by nature it is an extraordinarily open-ended and versatile intellectual resource. It reflects what Keats once referred to as "negative capability"—the capacity to encounter uncertainties, mysteries, and doubts "without an irritable reaching after fact & reason"—and it relies on many different ways of knowing. Thus there can be any number of approaches to the classic, whether as a book of divination or as a source of philosophical, spiritual, or psychological inspiration. The editors of China's most important premodern literary compilation, the *Complete Collection of the Four Treasuries*, re-marked in the eighteenth century that interpreting the *Changes* was like playing chess: no two games are alike, and there are infinite possibilities. Chinese scholars have identified literally hundreds of interpretive traditions focused on the *Yijing* in imperial times alone.

As indicated above, the judgment (sometimes described as a "hexagram statement," "decision," or "tag") suggests the overall meaning of the hexagram, in particular its powers and possibilities. The six lines of each hexagram represent a situation in time and space, a "field of action with multiple actors or factors," all of which are in constant, dynamic play.[2] The lines, read from bottom to top, represent the evolution of this situation and/or the major players involved. The first, second, and third lines constitute a "lower" trigram, and the fourth, fifth, and sixth lines form an "upper" trigram, each having its own set of primary and secondary symbolic attributes. Interpretation involves an understanding of the relationships among the lines, line statements, and trigrams of the chosen hexagram, and often an appreciation of the way in which the selected hexagram is related to other hexagrams. Commentaries of every conceivable sort have historically provided guidance in negotiating a path to understanding.

I have chosen the Gen hexagram—variously translated as Mountain, Restraint, Keeping Still, Bound, Stabilizing, Limited, Immobile, Steadiness, and the like[3]—as my primary example of hexagram analysis throughout this biography, not only because many

Chinese scholars, past and present, have considered it to capture the essence of the *Yijing*, but also because it had particularly wide appeal as an object of contemplation for Confucians, Buddhists, and Daoists alike. Below is a general description of Gen, based on a well-known set of Chinese commentaries.

Gen

The image of this hexagram is the mountain, the youngest son of Heaven and Earth. The solid line at the top represents the *yang* (active) principle, because it strives upward by nature. The broken line at the bottom represents the *yin* (passive) principle, since the direction of its movement is downward. Thus there is rest because the movement has come to a normal end. In its application to man, this hexagram turns on the problem of achieving a quiet heart and mind. It is very difficult to bring quiet to the heart and mind. Although Buddhism strives for rest through an ebbing away of all movement, the *Changes* holds that rest is merely part of a polarity that always posits movement as its complement.... True quiet means keeping still when the time has come to keep still, and going forward when the time has come to go forward.... When a man has become calm, he may turn to the outside world. He no longer sees in it the struggle and tumult of individual beings, and therefore he has that true peace of mind that is needed for understanding the great laws of the universe and for acting in harmony with them. Whoever acts from these deep levels of understanding makes no mistakes.[4]

The judgment of the Gen hexagram may be translated: "Keeping his back still he no longer feels his body. He goes into his courtyard and does not see his people. No blame." Although commentaries on this judgment vary widely, the general idea seems to be that the person to whom the hexagram refers—finding himself in the sort of situation that the hexagram describes—must calm his mind, conquer his emotions, and not be swayed by either his own ego or outside influences in making decisions and responding to changing circumstances. According to some commentators, the judgment refers to the effort by King Wen (ca. 1100–1050 BCE), founder of the Zhou dynasty, to withdraw from activity at a critical time in the consolidation of his regime, sitting in stillness while contemplating the future. The six lines of the hexagram, then, describe the stages of this contemplative process.

Generally speaking, the line statement of the first (bottom) line of the Gen hexagram indicates the need to take stock at the very beginning of a situation, without rushing into it precipitously. The second line statement warns against the dangers of being swept into action by powerful forces. The third line statement advises calmness and self-control, which must develop naturally and not be imposed artificially. The fourth line statement describes a situation in which the subject is making progress but has not yet conquered his egotistical drives and desires. The fifth line statement refers to the need for the subject to be cautious in what he says and to know when to speak and when to remain silent. The sixth line statement marks the attainment of equanimity and insight, thus facilitating success in all things.[5] Lest this seem like a simple process, it should be noted that in imperial China it was not uncommon for a scholar to spend days or even weeks contemplating a single hexagram. The reasons for this will become apparent as we proceed through the life of the *Yijing*.

The Transnational Travels of the *Changes*

The *Yijing*'s great prestige and multifaceted cultural role in China naturally commended it to several civilizations on the Chinese periphery—notably Korea, Japan, and Vietnam—each of which had long been influenced significantly by Chinese philosophy, religion, art, literature, and social customs. In all these environments, the *Changes* enjoyed an exalted reputation, and in each it was employed in a variety of cultural realms, as it had been in China. The process of transmission in East Asia was relatively uncomplicated—in part because the classical Chinese language in which the *Yijing* was written served as the literary lingua franca of virtually all educated Korean, Japanese, and Vietnamese elites until the late nineteenth century. Despite this powerful cultural common denominator, however, over time the *Changes* came to be used and understood in ways that reflected the particular needs and interests of the host environment, and in the process the *Yijing* became domesticated.

Similar processes of appropriation and adaptation took place much later in the West, but for somewhat different reasons and with sometimes radically different results. First, the *Yijing* had to be translated into various Western languages by scholars who had different levels of language ability and different political, religious, or personal agendas. In East Asia the *Changes* remained part of the dominant culture into the twentieth century, whereas in Europe and the Americas, particularly during the 1960s and 1970s, the radical otherness of the *Yijing* led to its use primarily as a countercultural document. To be sure, some individuals—Christian missionaries in particular—tried to find affinities between the *Changes* and the Bible, and scholars of various sorts sought to understand the document on its own terms, as a historical artifact rather than a living document. But on the whole the *Yijing* served in the West as a tool for challenging the establishment rather than supporting it.

The *Yijing* has touched many realms of modern Western culture, from the psychology of Carl G. Jung to the architecture of I. M. Pei. The choreographers Merce Cunningham and Carolyn Carlson have found inspiration in the *Changes*, as have such noted composers as Joseph Hauer, John Cage, Udo Kasemets, and James Tenney. It has been a significant element in the art of individuals such as William Littlefield, Eric Morris, Arnaldo Coen, Arturo Rivera, Augusto Ramírez, and Felipe Erenberg, and in the writings of a wide range of Western authors, including Philip K. Dick, Allen Ginsberg, Octavio Paz, Herman Hesse, Raymond Queneau, and Jorge Luis Borges. The practices of fengshui and Traditional Chinese Medicine (TCM), which have attracted so much attention around the world in recent decades, have their conceptual roots in, and derive much of their analytical and symbolic vocabulary from, the *Classic of Changes*.

A Brief Overview

My goal in this biography is to trace the evolution of the *Yijing* across space and time, and to account for its broad reach and sustained appeal, not only in the country of its birth but also in distant and dissimilar lands. My account begins with a chapter describing the origins of the *Changes*, focusing on the mythology that surrounds the document, its early structure and functions, and the way in which the basic text reflects the values and preoccupations of Bronze Age China. It also discusses competing versions of the *Yijing*.

The second chapter addresses the process by which the *Changes* became a Chinese classic in 136 BCE, giving special attention to the role of the Ten Wings in providing the document with a coherent cosmological framework and in expanding dramatically the interpretive possibilities of its hexagrams, trigrams, and lines. Chapter 2 also offers a brief comparison between the version of the *Yijing* that was fixed in 136 BCE (see the list of hexagrams at the beginning of this book) and competing versions, notably the so-called Mawangdui manuscript, discovered in 1973.

Chapter 3 consists of two parts. The first part explores a few of the many ways that Chinese commentators have approached the *Changes* from the second century BCE to the present. This discussion not only underscores the enormous complexity of *Yijing* interpretation; it also identifies and explains the numerical and other forms of correlative logic that so often informed it, suggesting, at least implicitly, comparisons with the kabbala and other mystical approaches to sacred texts. The second part focuses on the divinatory role of the *Changes* in Chinese society, giving attention to the rituals accompanying it, certain basic patterns of interpretation, and some specific examples of actual divinations undertaken by emperors, officials, scholars, and professional fortune-tellers.

The next two chapters address the travels of the *Yijing* and the transformations it underwent. Chapter 4 looks at the reception of the document in Japan, Korea, Vietnam, and Tibet, illustrating the various cultural uses to which it was put, as well as the sometimes substantial modifications it experienced over time. Chapter 5 examines the problems of translation that arose when advocates of the *Changes* sought to introduce the Chinese classic to Western audiences. A common feature of this process has been acute scholarly rivalry, often marked by acrimonious critiques leveled by translators against their predecessors and contemporary competitors. The chapter ends with a few examples of how the *Yijing* has found its way into Western culture, first as an alternative to mainstream culture and then as a commercial product of it.

My brief concluding remarks are designed to show why the *Changes* deserves to be considered one of the great works of world literature, on a par with such religious classics as the Bible, the Talmud, the Qur'an, the Bhagavad Gita, and the Lotus Sutra. The criteria include similarities in evolution, longevity, domestic significance, and global spread.

The Domestic Evolution of the *Yijing*

PART ONE

What makes a classic? First, the work must focus on matters of great importance, identifying fundamental human problems and providing some sort of guidance for dealing with them. Second, it must address these fundamental issues in "beautiful, moving, and memorable ways," with "stimulating and inviting images." Third, it must be complex, nuanced, comprehensive, and profound, requiring careful and repeated study in order to yield its deepest secrets and greatest wisdom. One might add that precisely because of these characteristics, a classic has great staying power across both space and time. By these criteria, and by most other measures as well, the *Yijing* certainly fits the bill.[1]

And yet it seems so different from other "classics" that instantly come to mind, whether literary works such as the *Odyssey*, the *Republic*, the *Divine Comedy*, and *The Pilgrim's Progress* or sacred scriptures like the Jewish and Christian Bibles, the Qur'an, the Hindu Vedas and the Buddhist sutras. Structurally it lacks any sort of systematic or sustained narrative, and from the standpoint of spirituality, it offers no vision of religious salvation, much less the promise of an afterlife or even the idea of rebirth.

According to Chinese tradition, the *Yijing* was based on the natural observations of the ancient sages; the cosmic order or Dao that it expressed had no Creator or Supreme Ordainer, much less a host of good and malevolent deities to exert influence in various ways. There is no jealous and angry God in it; no evil presence like Satan; no prophet, sinner, or savior; no story of floods or plagues; no tale of people swallowed up by whales or turned into pillars of salt. The *Changes* posits neither a purposeful beginning nor an apocalyptic end; and whereas classics such as the Bible and Qur'an insist that humans are answerable not to their own culture but to a being that transcends all culture, the *Yijing* takes essentially the opposite position. One might add that in the Western tradition, God reveals only what God chooses to reveal, while in traditional China, the "mind of Heaven" was considered ultimately knowable and accessible through the *Changes*. The "absolute gulf between God and his creatures" in the West had no counterpart in the Chinese tradition.[2]

Yet despite its brevity, cryptic text, paucity of colorful stories, virtual absence of deities, and lack of a sustained narrative, the *Yijing* exerted enormous influence in all realms of Chinese culture for well over two thousand years—an influence comparable to the Bible in Judeo-Christian culture, the Qur'an in Islamic culture, the Vedas in Hindu culture, and the sutras in Buddhist culture. What was so appealing about the document, and why was it so influential?

Genesis of the *Changes*

We often cannot say exactly when, where, or how ancient texts were born. Some of the reasons are obvious. The further away in time, the more likely a work's origins will be obscure: memories fade, original materials disappear, alternative versions surface. Often, not least in the case of many of the world's most sacred texts, diverse materials have accumulated over long periods, edited by different hands under different historical conditions. This is true, to a greater or lesser degree, of the Hebrew Bible (known, with some rearrangement of material, as the Old Testament), the Qur'an, the Hindu Vedas, and the early recorded pronouncements of Siddhartha, the historic Buddha. It is also true of the *Zhou Changes*, which, when sanctioned as a foundational text by the Chinese state in 136 BCE, became the *Classic of Changes*, or *Yijing*.

Myths and Histories

According to a prominent Chinese legend, a great culture hero named Fuxi invented a set of eight three-line symbols known as trigrams, which became the foundation of the *Changes*. The basic story reads like this:

> When in ancient times Lord Baoxi [Fuxi] ruled the world as sovereign, he looked upward and observed the images in heaven and looked downward and observed the models that the earth provided. He observed the patterns on birds and beasts and what things were suitable for the land. Nearby, adopting them from his own person, and afar, adopting them from other things, he thereupon made the eight trigrams in order to become thoroughly conversant with the virtues inherent in the numinous and the bright and to classify the myriad things in terms of their true, innate natures.[1]

By this account Fuxi was able to represent by means of the eight trigrams a rudimentary but comprehensive understanding of the fundamental order of the universe.

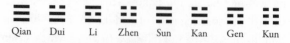

Qian   Dui   Li   Zhen   Sun   Kan   Gen   Kun

Later, we are told, these eight trigrams came to be doubled, creating a total of sixty-four six-line figures called hexagrams, each with a one- or two-character name that described its fundamental symbolism. Some legends give Fuxi credit for this development; others suggest that another mythological personality, Shennong, may have devised the sixty-four hexagrams. Still other accounts assert that a fully historical figure, King

Wen, founder of the Zhou dynasty (ca. 1045–256 BCE), invented the hexagrams and put them in what became their conventional order in 136 BCE. King Wen is also often credited with attaching to each hexagram the short explanatory texts known as judgments, and for adding to each individual line a line statement indicating its symbolic significance within the structure of each hexagram. Some sources claim that King Wen's son, the Duke of Zhou, added the line statements, and much later Confucius (551–479 BCE) reportedly added the set of commentaries known collectively as the Ten Wings.

One or another version of this general narrative served for more than two thousand years as the commonly accepted explanation for how the *Yijing* evolved. The archaeological evidence, however, tells a rather different tale.

Trigrams and hexagrams seem to have developed from very early forms of Chinese numerology, including those associated with oracle bone divination—a Shang dynasty (ca. 1600–ca. 1050 BCE) royal practice. By applying intense heat to the dried plastrons of turtles and the scapulae of cattle—a technique sometimes known as pyromancy—the late Shang and early Zhou kings and their priestly diviners were able to produce cracks in the bone, which yielded answers to questions dealing with topics such as family matters, sacrifice, travel, warfare, hunting and fishing, and settlement planning. The "questions" were normally phrased as prayerlike declarations or proposals, the correctness of which could then be tested by divination(s). Written inscriptions carved into a great many of these oracle bones provide direct evidence of the issues the kings addressed as well as the outcomes of their divinations.[2]

So far archaeological excavations in China have yielded more oracle bones and bronzes with numerical inscriptions that indicate hexagrams than those that indicate trigrams; thus it is at least possible that the latter were derived from the former rather than the reverse, contrary to the common myth. Some scholars have suggested that as early as the twelfth or eleventh century BCE, Shang dynasty diviners may already have begun to analyze trigram and hexagram relationships in terms of techniques previously thought to date only from the final centuries of the Zhou dynasty or later, while others have argued that at least some of the numerical hexagrams found on oracle bones and bronzes are not related to the conventional divinatory traditions of the *Changes* at all.

Much debate surrounds the issue of when and why various sets of odd and even numbers became "hexagram pictures" with solid and broken lines, and at what point written statements came to be attached to these lines. A good guess is that a more or less complete early version of the basic text of the *Changes* emerged in China no later than about 800 BCE.[3] Recent archaeological discoveries have shown, however, that there were several different traditions of *Yijing*-related divination in the latter part of the Zhou period, and that hexagram pictures and divinatory procedures took a variety of forms in different localities and at different times.

Some authorities believe that the solid lines of trigrams and hexagrams represent single-segment bamboo sticks used in divination, while broken lines represent double-segmented sticks. Others have suggested an early system of calculation based on knotted cords, in which a big knot signified a solid line and two smaller knots signified a broken line. Still others have argued that the eight trigrams were originally derived either from the cracks in oracle bones or from pictographs of certain key words or concepts that came to be associated with them. Yet another generative possibility may be a rudimentary sexual symbolism. It is difficult even for non-Freudians to look at the first two hexagrams in the received order—Qian and Kun, respectively—and not see representations of a penis and a vulva.

Qian   Kun

We do not know for certain what the numerically generated trigrams and hexagrams in late Shang and early Zhou oracle bones and other sources might have signified, but by the middle or late Zhou period the primary meanings of the eight trigrams seem to have stabilized (see below). No later than the fourth century, probably earlier, additional meanings began to be attached to these trigrams—meanings that would later become part of an important commentary to the basic text called "Explaining the Trigrams."

Qian	Dui	Li	Zhen	Sun	Kan	Gen	Kun
Heaven	Lake	Fire	Thunder	Wind	Water	Mountain	Earth

As for the sixty-four hexagrams, we know only that at some point during the early Zhou period—probably about 800 BCE, but perhaps earlier—each of them acquired a name referring to a thing, an activity, a state, a situation, a quality, an emotion, or a relationship; for example, "Well," "Cauldron," "Marrying Maid," "Treading," "Following," "Viewing," "Juvenile Ignorance," "Peace," "Obstruction," "Waiting," "Contention," "Ills to be Cured," "Modesty," "Elegance," "Great Strength," "Contentment," "Inner Trust," "Joy," "Closeness," "Fellowship," "Reciprocity."[4] There has always been a great deal of debate, however, about the order in which these hexagrams originally appeared, and about the early meanings of the hexagram names and their variants.[5]

In the conventional version of the *Yijing*, which may well represent the earliest order of the hexagrams, they are organized into pairs according to one of two principles, each of which involves opposition: The primary organizing principle is one of inversion, by which one hexagram becomes its opposite by virtue of being turned upside down. Fifty-six of the hexagrams fall into this category. The remaining eight, in which inversion would not produce a change, are joined by the principle of lateral linkage—that is, a hexagram structure that would emerge if each line of the original hexagram turned into its opposite.

Tai   Pi

Yi   Daguo

Most hexagram names in the *Changes* seem to have been derived from a term or concept that appears in their respective judgments or individual line statements. Take, for example, Gen (number 52 in the conventional order), discussed briefly in the introduction and at greater length below and in subsequent chapters. In this hexagram the character *gen* appears not only in the judgment but also in all six line statements.[6]

Here is what one early Zhou dynasty understanding of the judgment and the individual line statements of Gen might have been:

Gen
艮

JUDGMENT: If one cleaves the back he will not get hold of the body; if one goes into the courtyard he will not see the person. There will be no misfortune.

(艮其背不獲其身行其庭不見人无咎)

First (bottom) line: Cleave the feet. There will be no misfortune. Favorable in a long-range determination.

(艮其趾无咎利永貞)

Second line: Cleave the lower legs, but don't re-
move the bone marrow. His heart is not
pleased.

(艮其腓不拯其隨其心不快)

Third line: Cleave the waist, rend the spinal meat.
It is threatening. Smoke the heart.

(艮其限列其夤厲薰心)

Fourth line: Cleave the torso [lit., body]. There
will be no misfortune.

(艮其身无咎)

Fifth line: Cleave the jaw. Talk will be orderly.
Troubles will go away.

(艮其輔言有序悔亡)

Sixth line: Cleave thickly. Auspicious.

(敦艮吉)[7]

Another possible verbal meaning of *gen* in this particular hexagram is "to glare at," which would, of course,
fundamentally change the meaning of each line.[8]

As is apparent from this example, many hexagram
judgments are extremely cryptic and subject to any
number of interpretations. About 70 percent of them
refer to ancient and now obscure divinatory formulas
involving sacrifices or offerings to spirits.[9] Here are a
few examples of such formulas:

Qian (number 1 in the received order): "Primary
receipt, favorable to divine."

Shi (number 7): "The determination is favorable
for a great man; no misfortune."

Lü (number 10): "Step on the tiger's tail; it won't bite the person; a sacrificial offering."

Tongren (number 13): "Gather the people in the open country; a sacrificial offering; favorable for crossing a big river; a favorable determination for a noble person."

Dayou (number 14): "A great harvest; a grand offering."

Qian (number 15): "An offering; for a noble person there will be a conclusion."

Shike (number 21): "An offering; favorable for resolving a legal dispute."

Bo (number 23): "Not favorable when there is somewhere to go."

Longer judgments generally provide variations on the same or similar themes. For instance, Kun (number 2) reads: "Primary receipt. A determination favorable for a mare. A noble man who is going somewhere will first lose his way, and later find a host. Favorable to the west and south, one will find a friend; to the east and north, one will lose a friend. Auspicious in a determination about security." Fu (number 24) reads: "An offering; in going out and coming in there will be no illness. A friend will arrive without misfortune; he will turn around and head back on his way, and return in seven days. Favorable for having somewhere to go." One can easily see how such statements might lend themselves to a variety of interpretations, even if originally they referred to very specific circumstances.

Like judgments, the individual line statements of the hexagrams—which vary in length from as few as two characters to as many as thirty—often include records from previous divinations that were either transmitted orally or recorded in early divination manuals of one kind or another. Many of these statements seem to be based directly or indirectly on "omen verses" of the sort that can also be found on Shang dynasty oracle bones. Here are a few examples of line statements that happen to deal explicitly with the theme of military affairs: Line 5 of Shi (number 7): "In the hunt there is a catch: advantageous to shackle captives; no misfortune. The elder son leads the troops; the younger son carts the corpses; the determination is ominous." Line 3 of Lü (number 10): "The feeble-sighted will be able to see; the lame will be able to walk. Step on a tiger's tail; it will bite the person. Ominous. A warrior performs for the great ruler." Line 6 of Fu (number 24): "Lost return; ominous; there will be a calamity. If troops are set in motion, there will be a great defeat. For the ruler of the state there will be a calamity; for up to ten years it will not be possible to launch a military campaign."

As with the judgments, most line statements that contain explicitly divinatory material indicate positive prognostications or the nonjudgmental expression "no harm/misfortune." The most common negative terms in the *Changes*—"regret," "remorse," "distress," "threatening," and "ominous"—appear only about 130 times in the judgments and line statements, compared to about 430 instances of "auspicious," "favorable," "advantageous," or "successful."[10] Other fairly frequent divinatory terms, such as "to put something to use" (55 occurrences), also have positive connotations.

As should be readily apparent, commentaries have long been necessary to make sense of the cryptic utterances reflected in so many hexagram judgments and line statements. Indeed, over the past two millennia or so, virtually every one of the four thousand-plus substantive words in the basic text has been subjected to intense and relentless scrutiny.

Many passages from the *Changes* have been interpreted in widely disparate ways. The reasons for this diversity of opinion are not difficult to find. In the first place, the divinations recorded in the *Changes* usually lack sufficient context, inviting sometimes wild speculations. Ancient terms and allusions are often unclear; loan words, local variants, and scribal errors abound. Moreover, after the rise of Confucianism and other moralistic philosophies from about the sixth century BCE onward, simple value-neutral descriptions of events that appeared in the judgments and line statements of the "original" *Changes* increasingly became prescriptions for proper behavior: "dids" became "shoulds," so to speak.

As part of the process, a number of obscure or unsettling terms and phrases came to be understood in new ways. Thus a term like *fu*, which originally seems to have denoted "capture" or a "captive" in war, came increasingly to be understood as a moral quality: "sincerity" or "trustworthiness." Similarly the term *heng*, which originally had to do with the specific ritual sacrifices surrounding a divination, came to be glossed as "prevalence," "success," or "penetrating." *Zhen*, originally denoting a "determination" of some sort, came to be interpreted as "constancy," "perseverance," or "correctness and firmness."

Other Prominent Features
of the Original *Changes*

Linguistic devices such as rhyme, alliteration, and the pairing of opposite ideas, which initially facilitated the memorization and transmission of prognostications, invested the line statements of the *Changes* with a powerful "word magic," especially after they were rendered into writing.[11] Roughly a third of the basic text contains rhymes of one sort or another. In some places entire phrases are rhymed; in others internal rhymes are more prevalent. An apt illustration is the Kun hexagram (number 2), in which the second word in five of its six major line statements is rhymed.

About twenty hexagrams have extensive rhyming schemes, and another thirty or so contain at least some rhymes. Many line statements also display plays on words and double entendres, which, like rhymes and alliterations, are almost invariably lost in translation.[12] Among the numerous two-character juxtapositions in the basic text, we find contrasts such as presence and absence, loss and gain, bright and dark, sweet and bitter, big and small, up and down, level and slope, auspicious and ominous, going and coming, advance and retreat, beginning and ending, inside and outside, weeping and laughing, vassal and ruler, traveler and townsperson, older and younger, and tying and untying. These contrasts suggest a possible source of inspiration for the complementary qualities that later came to be associated with *yin* and *yang*. Although these two concepts are not identified as such in the earliest strata of the *Changes*, they are unmistakably manifest in the late Zhou dynasty commentaries that became known as the Ten Wings.

Another prominent feature of the early *Changes* is the way that many of its judgments and line statements concentrate certain kinds of information. For example, the third, fourth, and fifth lines of the hexagram known as Daxu or Dachu (conventionally translated "Great Domestication," number 26) refer to a horse, an ox, and a pig, respectively. There are similar concentrations of information in hexagrams such as Shi ("The Army," number 7, which deals with military affairs), Tongren ("Fellowship," number 13, concerned specifically with fighting), Fu ("Return," number 24, focused on travel), and Daguo ("Major Superiority," number 28, containing botanical lore).

Some hexagrams present their information spatially as well as topically. Consider, for example, Jian (number 53):

Line 1: The wild goose advances to the riverbank; threatening for a small child. There will be talk. No misfortune.

Line 2: The wild goose advances to a boulder. It eats and drinks and goes "honk honk." Auspicious.

Line 3: The wild goose advances to the high ground. The husband goes on a military campaign and does not return. The wife is pregnant but does not give birth. Ominous.

Line 4: The wild goose advances to the trees. Someone will get his perch. There will be no misfortune.

Line 5: The wild goose advances to a ridge. The wife does not become pregnant for three years. In the end, nothing overcomes it. Auspicious.

Line 6: The wild goose advances to high ground; its feathers can be used as an emblem [in a dance?]. Auspicious.[13]

Other such spatially oriented hexagrams include Qian (number 1), Xian (number 31), and Gen (number 52).

One of the most important structural features of the early *Changes*, and one that has received an enormous amount of commentarial attention throughout the centuries, has to do with the way that certain phrases in the line statements are repeated in two or more hexagrams. There are many examples of such shared utterances. Some are general prognostications: "Ominous for an attack," for instance, occurs in the line statements of no less than ten hexagrams. Others are time notations: "Seven days," for example, appears in the line statements of at least three hexagrams. Sometimes hexagrams are linked by oppositional line statements. In the Lü hexagram (number 56), we encounter the phrase "he gets his money-axes"; in the Sun hexagram (number 57), "he loses his money-axes." In the Tongren hexagram (number 13), the subject of the fifth line first cries out and then laughs, while in the sixth line of Lü (number 56), the subject first laughs and then cries out.

Of particular interest to Chinese commentators have been shared lines or phrases in hexagrams that seem to be related structurally. For instance, the statement for the fourth line of Kuai (also known as Guai, number 43) contains exactly the same phrase—"with no skin on the buttocks, his walking is labored"—as the third line of Gou (number 44). Gou is the hexagram that would result if Kuai were turned upside down (at which point, of course, the fourth line of Kuai would become the third line of Gou). Similarly, line 3 in Jiji (number 63) and line 4 in Weiji (number 64) both refer to attacks on the Gui border state. There are several other instances of this type of relationship, indicating, it would appear, a conscious effort at correlation. Over the years, as we shall see, efforts by scholars and diviners to find creative ways of linking line statements with hexagram structures generated a great number of different systems involving the general idea of "hexagram changes."

The Cultural Content of the Early *Changes*

Chinese scholars have long debated the basic nature of the *Yijing*. Some consider it to be nothing more than a divination manual, while others have described it as a book of philosophy, a historical work, an ancient dictionary or encyclopedia, an early scientific treatise, and even a mathematical model of the universe. Certain claims are easier to sustain than others, but it is clear in any case that the basic text of the *Changes* has much to tell us about the perceptions and preoccupations of both elites and commoners in late Shang and early Zhou dynasty China.

The vast world of ancestral and other spirits in Bronze Age China is implicit in the divinations, sacrifices, and prayers that suffuse the basic text of the *Changes*. But there are only a few explicit references to ghosts and spirits. Shangdi, the spiritual "Lord on High" of the Shang people, is mentioned only once in the basic text by name, and the spiritual power known as Tian or "Heaven" appears infrequently as such. On the other hand, the majority of hexagram judgments contain at least one reference to sacrifices, and some hexagrams—notably Lin (number 19), Guan (number 20), Xian (number 31), Gen (number 52), and Huan (number 59)—display a preoccupation with them, including some particularly gory details concerning the dismemberment of both animals and human war captives for ritual purposes. Here, for example, are the judgment and line statements of Xian, which seems to parallel Gen in certain respects:

> JUDGMENT: Sacrificial offering; a favorable determination. Auspicious for taking a maiden as a wife.
> Line 1: Cut [off?] the big toes [of the sacrificial victim].
> Line 2: Cut the lower legs; ominous. Auspicious for dwellings.
> Line 3: Cut the thighs. Take hold of the bone marrow. To go will be distressing.
> Line 4: The determination is auspicious. Troubles will go away. You feel unsettled and go back and forth: a friend is following your thoughts.
> Line 5: Cut the spinal flesh. No trouble.
> Line 6: Cut the cheeks, jowls, and tongue.[14]

The basic text of the *Changes* reflects the sharp social divide between members of the aristocratic elite ("noble people" and "great men") and commoners ("small people"). Later the term "noble people" (lit., "sons of lords") would come to signify those with exemplary moral qualities, just as the term "small people" would come to mean selfish and petty persons. But in the earliest strata of the *Changes*, these are purely social distinctions. Virtually all sectors and strata of society are represented in the line statements: men, women, and children; husbands, wives, and concubines; farmers, merchants, bondservants, servants, bandits, priests, and magicians. In daily life there are births and burials; people lose things and gain things; they get sick and recover or die; they laugh and giggle; they sigh, cry, and sob (sometimes with snivel and snot); they moan and groan; and they cower in terror.

The economic world described in the basic text is primarily a pastoral and hunting one. There are no references to the sea and relatively few to the cultivation of crops—but many to hunting, herding, fishing, gathering plants, and raising livestock. There are several references to barbarians and to brutal and bloody punishments of various sorts, usually for unspecified crimes. As indicated above, tribal warfare and the taking of prisoners for slave labor or human sacrifice was a prominent characteristic of Shang society, and although ritualized human sacrifice diminished during the early Zhou period, recent archaeological discoveries indicate that it was still practiced.[15]

Not surprisingly, nature looms large in the earliest layers of the *Changes*. Several hexagrams refer explicitly to astronomical or calendrical phenomena, including Kui (number 38) and Feng (number 55). References in the former to foxes, swine, and ghosts pertain to celestial objects and configurations rather than terrestrial beings, and references in the latter to observances of the Dipper at midday suggest a solar eclipse. One of the most interesting instances of astronomical imagery in the *Yijing* appears in the line statements of Qian (number 1), which boasts an extra statement (as does Kun, number 2). The text reads:

> Line 1: A submerged dragon; don't use [the outcome of this determination].
>
> Line 2: A dragon sighted in a field; it will be favorable to see a great man.
>
> Line 3: The noble person throughout the day is vigorous, but at night he is wary; threatening but there will be no misfortune.
>
> Line 4: Sometimes [the dragon] leaps in the deep; no misfortune.
>
> Line 5: A dragon flying in the sky: it will be favorable to see a great man.
>
> Line 6: A gorged dragon: there will be trouble.
>
> Extra line: Seeing a group of dragons without heads: auspicious.[16]

Although on first blush the Qian hexagram seems to be concerned with the activities of a mythical beast,[17] its focus is actually calendrical, and the imagery is, in fact, astronomical. That is, the dragon in the statements refers to a Chinese constellation named Canlong (lit., Blue-Green Dragon), which was "submerged" under the eastern horizon during the winter. It appeared just above the horizon in spring, extended fully across the sky in summer, and descended head-first beneath the western horizon at the autumnal equinox.[18] The original symbolism, then, was seasonal: Qian represented the birth of things in the spring, their growth during the summer, and their maturity (and harvest) in the fall. Later the activities of the dragon as depicted in the Qian hexagram came to be widely understood as the actions appropriate to the "superior man" or "exemplary person"—another instance of transformed imagery.

Many of the line statements and judgments of the *Changes* describe objects and processes of nature: thunder and lightning, clouds, wind and rain, earth and fire; mountains, lakes, pools, rivers, rocks, trees, fruits, vines, and flowers. There are also animals of all sorts (some of which are described as mating), from supernatural beasts to both wild and domestic animals, including deer, foxes, birds of all kinds, pigs and piglets, horses, fish, pheasants, geese, tigers, leopards, elephants, goats, turtles, and rodents. Material objects mentioned in the line statements include gold, silk, jade, talismans, cowry shells, clothing, liquor, houses, food products, flasks, tureens, eating utensils, musical instruments, sacrificial altars and ritual vessels, wagons, carts, shoes, weapons, and various household items.

The *Yijing* also contains a significant number of personal and place names, titles, and historical allusions. Indeed, some traditional Chinese accounts of the *Changes*—and some recent Western ones as well—see in the work a "hidden history" of the late Shang and early Zhou dynasties.[19] A close analysis of the line statements of the final two hexagrams of the conventional text reveals, for example, unmistakable references to the military activities of King Wu Ding (ca.

1200 BCE) of the Shang, and less obvious but still evident references to the Zhou dynasty's desire to legitimate itself as the rightful successor to the Shang. This does not mean, however, that we can accept at face value all claims for the antiquity of the basic text. Despite tantalizing bits of evidence, it remains doubtful that King Wen wrote the judgments or the line statements of the received version of the *Yijing*.

Early Uses of the *Changes*

The *Yijing* began its life in China as a book of divination. The numbers that yielded hexagrams were derived from the manipulation of stalks of the dried milfoil plant (*Achillea millefolium*), also known as yarrow. We do not know, however, how the stalks were originally manipulated. All that can be said with confidence is that a hexagram was initially chosen by some numerical means, through manipulation of the milfoil stalks, and that a particular line was usually singled out for emphasis, perhaps in a process distinct from, but related to, the one that yielded the hexagram in the first place.

The most complete written records of *Yijing*-based divination in the Zhou dynasty come from the *Zuo Commentary*, a highly influential work dating from around the late fourth century BCE that was designed to explicate an extraordinarily brief and cryptic text known as the *Spring and Autumn Annals*. The *Zuo*

Commentary provides about two dozen fairly detailed examples of how the *Changes* came to be used during the so-called Spring and Autumn period—specifically, from 672 to 485 BCE. Although it says nothing about the process by which hexagrams were generated, the text nonetheless allows us to discern certain significant patterns of interpretation as well as important changes in the way the *Yijing* was used over time.

There were four basic stages in early *Changes* divination according to the *Zuo Commentary*: first, a topic was proposed; second, a diviner was consulted; third, a stalk-casting process identified a particular hexagram to be examined; and finally, an expert (who may or may not have been the diviner) interpreted the results. Interpretations of this sort involved analyzing one or more of the constituent elements of the hexagram(s) under consideration—hexagram names, judgments, line statements, and especially trigram relationships. A constant feature of *Changes* interpretation throughout the Spring and Autumn period seems to be that it was "a rather ad hoc affair," involving practices that were "multiple and often contradictory."[20] Later interpreters of the *Yijing* likewise enjoyed extraordinary latitude in their effort to make meaning out of its cryptic judgments, line statements, and trigram configurations.

The earliest stories of *Yijing*-based divinations in the *Zuo Commentary* indicate that a specific line came to be identified by a procedure in which one hexagram—however it might have been generated—was paired with another hexagram that differed in structure only by a single line. For example, to identify the interpretive importance of the fourth line of the Guan hexagram (number 20), the diviner would refer to "Guan's Pi," since the only structural difference between Guan and the Pi hexagram (number 12) is the fourth line, which is broken in Guan and solid in Pi (see below). An understanding of the line statement might then be facilitated by an analysis of the trigram symbolism of one or both hexagrams.

Guan   Pi

Here is an example, dating from 672 BCE, in which Marquis Li of the Chen state requested a divination about the prospects for his son, Jingzhong, to become a ruler:

> [The diviner] encountered Guan's Pi and he remarked, "The [fourth line statement of Guan] says, 'Beholding the light of the state / It is beneficial to be the king's guest.'" In interpreting these two rhymed passages, the diviner explained that Kun, the lower trigram of the Guan and Pi hexagrams, represented the land; Sun, the upper trigram of Guan, represented the wind; and Qian, the upper trigram of Pi, represented the heavens. Wind rising above the earth to the heavens symbolized a mountain, and thus "If the treasures of the mountain are illuminated by the light of heaven, then he [Jingzhong, the Marquis' son] will occupy the land."[21]

Another example of early Zhou hexagram analysis is the story of Duke Mu of Qin's punitive expedition against Duke Hui of Jin in 645 BCE. Before the attack Duke Mu asked his diviner, Tufu, to consult the *Changes* regarding the outcome. Tufu selected the hexagram Gu (number 18; see below). The judgment of this hexagram reads in part: "Favorable for crossing a big river." The diviner thus predicted victory (in apparently extemporaneous rhymed verse), remarking thereafter that Duke Mu's troops would cross the Yellow River separating Qin from Jin, defeat the forces of Duke Hui, and arrest the duke. He explained that since the inner (lower) trigram of Gu was Sun ("Wind") and the outer (upper) one was Gen ("Mountain"), the winds of Qin would blow down the "fruits" of Jin on the mountain and their assets would be seized.[22] That is, Qin would prevail in the struggle. Significantly, in this case and several others as well, the trigrams that figure in the prognostication have primary symbolic associations similar, if not identical, to those that generally prevailed in later periods.

Gu

From about 600 BCE onward, the *Changes* came to be used not only for divination but also for rhetorical effect. That is, individuals used quotations from the text to bolster their arguments, indicating increasing public access to the work and greater public awareness of it. The *Zuo Commentary* provides several illuminating examples of this rhetorical usage. Here is one, involving a conflict between the feudal states of Jin and Chu in 597 BCE. At the time, an impetuous and insubordinate Jin officer named Zhizi led his forces across a river to attack the enemy without waiting for orders; in response, one of his military colleagues remarked: "This army [of Zhizi] is in great danger! The *Changes* expresses the idea in Shi's Lin [i.e., the first line statement of the Shi hexagram, number 7 in the conventional order] that 'The army sets out according to regulations. If it does not preserve them, it will be inauspicious.'"[23] He follows this remark with a trigram analysis in which the "weakness" associated with Kun ("Earth"), the upper trigram in both the Shi and Lin hexagrams, and the "obstruction" associated with Dui ("Lake"), the lower trigram of Lin (number 19), combine to compromise the entire operation: "The regulations are not preserved." Furthermore, we learn that the Lin hexagram means "not doing [work that should be done]." As a consequence, the colleague avers, "if we encounter [the enemy], we will certainly be defeated. Zhizi has set it up. Even if he escapes and returns home, there will certainly be a great fault."

In this instance we have no indication that a divination was ever performed; what the text of the *Zuo Commentary* reveals is nothing more than a stinging critique of Zhizi's insubordination, using the moral authority of the *Changes* and employing the trigram symbolism of both the Shi and Lin hexagrams as a kind of parable.

Extant texts from the Warring States period (ca. 475–221 BCE) tend overwhelmingly to reflect the use of the *Changes* for rhetorical purposes, but it is clear that during this period the basic text and its variants continued to be widely employed in divination, reaching ever broader segments of the population in the process. This expanded use of the document in various forms and for various purposes is particularly evident in recent Chinese archaeological discoveries of *Yijing*-related materials written on silk and bamboo during the fourth and third centuries BCE. What these discoveries reveal in particular is that several significantly different versions of the *Changes* circulated in China during the two or three centuries prior to its designation as a classic in 136 BCE, and that the final version probably owes a considerable debt to interpretive traditions represented by these alternative texts.

Unfortunately the five major hexagram-based texts discovered since the 1970s exist only in fragments, and scholars are still trying to determine what their relationship might have been to the final version of the *Changes*. Many hexagram names are the same or similar, as are several line statements and judgments, but the order of the hexagrams, the spacing of the trigrams, and even the structure of the individual lines sometimes differ substantially. In certain texts hexagrams appear side by side rather than sequentially, and there are instances in which we find geometric symbols or written prognostications that have no counterpart in the final version of the *Changes*. Intriguingly, one set of bamboo slips unearthed in 1993 includes inscriptions dating from the third century BCE that match almost exactly certain extant fragments of a long-lost hexagram-based text known as the *Return to the Hidden*, which reportedly predates the *Changes*.[24]

The most complete and revealing early alternative to the final version of the *Changes* is the Mawangdui (Hunan province) silk manuscript, discovered in 1973 and dating no later than 168 BCE.[25] Although this manuscript is of great interest in its own right, for our purposes the most important feature of the document is the light it sheds on the complex process by which the *Changes* became a classic in 136 BCE. This process, still incompletely understood, involved the addition of a set of commentaries known collectively as the Ten Wings, which transformed a relatively simple divination manual into a sophisticated philosophical tract. What the Mawangdui manuscript tells us is that just decades before the *Changes* received canonical status, there was still no consensus on how to understand and use the basic text.

The Mawangdui manuscript is the only version of the *Changes* unearthed since the 1970s that contains a set of commentaries corresponding roughly to the Ten Wings. But, as with the order of the hexagrams in the Mawangdui basic text, these commentaries are organized in significantly different ways and include passages for which there are no counterparts in the received version of the *Yijing*. As one brief example, in the Mawangdui commentary known as the "The Properties [or Inner Concerns] of the *Changes*," we find a long conversation between Confucius and his disciple Zi Gong in which the Sage, after being challenged by his assertive pupil, claims that he values the *Changes* as a book of wisdom, not as a divination manual:

> Zi Gong said: "Does the Master also believe in milfoil divination?" The Master said: "I am right in [only] seventy out of one hundred prognostications.... As for the *Changes*, I do indeed put its prayers and divinations last, only observing its virtue and propriety.... The divinations of scribes and magicians tend toward virtue [through their examination of numbers] but are not yet there; [they] delight in it but they are not correct. Perhaps it will be because of the *Changes* that gentlemen of later generations will doubt me. I seek its virtue and nothing more. I am on the same road as the scribes and magicians but end up differently. The conduct of the gentleman's virtue is to seek blessings; that is why he sacrifices, but little. The righteousness of his humaneness is to seek auspiciousness; that is why he divines but rarely."[26]

This passage has occasioned a great deal of comment from Chinese and Western scholars, and while it seems clear that the Confucius represented here wants to emphasize that the *Yijing* is primarily a repository of ancient moral wisdom, his messages about prognostication seem quite mixed. In fact, in the passage immediately following the Sage's exchange with his challenging student, he remarks that "the enlightened lord does not for a moment or a night or a day or a month fail to divine by turtle shell or milfoil . . . [in order to know] auspiciousness and inauspiciousness and to comply with Heaven and Earth."[27]

The Making of a Classic

CHAPTER 2

Without the Ten Wings, it is extremely unlikely that the basic text of the *Changes* would have become anything more than a technical divination manual, one of many such documents circulating in the late Warring States period. But as it turned out, this particular collection of commentaries, which evolved over several centuries, proved ideally suited to the political, social, intellectual, and cultural climate of China during the long and distinguished reign of Emperor Wu of the Han dynasty (r. 141–87 BCE). In the first place, the Ten Wings reflected the eclecticism, cosmology, and "Confucian" values that came to be esteemed by Emperor Wu's scholarly advisers. But perhaps even more important, although the individual wings were quite heterogeneous and obviously the products of different periods and editorial hands, Chinese scholars in the second century BCE, including the Grand Historian, Sima Qian (ca. 145–86 BCE), ascribed them to Confucius (ca. 551–479 BCE). This now-questionable association with the Sage invested the basic text with great stature and encouraged Chinese scholars from the Han period onward to give the document particularly careful scrutiny, and to search relentlessly for the deeper significance of its hexagrams, trigrams, lines, judgments, line statements, and even individual words.

Late Zhou–Early Han Cosmology and the Ten Wings

One of the most important philosophical ideas to emerge out of the vibrant discussions and debates that took place in China during the fourth and third centuries BCE was the widely shared notion that the general goal of human activity was to harmonize with the natural patterns of change in the universe. How these patterns might be detected and understood, and what one might do to achieve this harmony, differed substantially among various schools and individual thinkers. But for many if not most Chinese intellectuals of the time, divination offered a useful, indeed essential, means by which to understand the cosmos and one's place in it. Naturally, then, the *Changes*, having originated as a fortune-telling manual, came increasingly to be viewed as a potentially valuable instrument for achieving this kind of understanding. At the same time, however, the basic text had very little to say explicitly about cosmic patterns and processes. Thus it became necessary to amplify the document in ways that took into account new and compelling ideas about the relationship among Heaven, Earth, and Humanity.

The concept of "Heaven" had evolved during the Zhou dynasty from a notion somewhat similar to the Shang dynasty's highly personalized "Lord on High" to a less personalized idea of nature and natural process, commonly referred to as the Way or Dao. Depending on one's philosophical persuasion, the Dao could be moral or amoral, but to virtually all Chinese thinkers of the late Zhou era, it possessed cosmic creative power without being itself a creator external to the cosmos.

Most of the cosmogonies of the late Zhou and early Han periods focused on the concept of multiplicity developing out of oneness. But the idea that eventually proved most powerful philosophically was the implicitly sexual interaction between Heaven (male) and Earth (female), which generated all phenomena. This process came to be viewed in terms of the (also implicitly sexual) interaction between yin and yang. Such sexual imagery was not always implicit, however. In the Mawangdui version of the *Changes*, for instance, the hexagrams that correspond to Qian ("Heaven") and Kun ("Earth") in the canonized version (Jian and Chuan, respectively) seem to be closely identified with male and female genitalia.[1]

From the late Zhou period onward, yin and yang came to be conceived in three different but related ways. First, they were viewed as modes of cosmic creativity (female and male, respectively), which not only produced but also animated all natural phenomena. Second, they were used to identify recurrent, cyclical patterns of rise (yang) and decline (yin), waxing (yang) and waning (yin). Third, they were employed as comparative categories, describing dualistic relationships that were viewed as inherently unequal but almost invariably complementary. Yang, for example, came to be associated with light, activity, Heaven, the sun, fire, heat, the color red, and roundness, while yin was correlated with Earth, the moon, water, coldness, the color black, and squareness, as well as darkness and passivity.

Significantly, objects or qualities that might be viewed as yang from one point of view can be seen as yin from another. For instance in figure 2.1, which shows detail from a delightful painting by Zhu Da (1624–1705), the large rock is yang, by virtue of not only predominance of light as opposed to shading but also the rock's "superior" position and its size in relation to the fish (who seems to be staring intently at it). Yet because the rock is stationary and the fish is presumably in motion, the rock can be considered yin. And although the staring fish is clearly yin in relation to the size of the rock, it is yang in relation to the smaller fish that is swimming away from it.

For objects such as rocks and fish to exist, for patterns of movement to be detected, and for relationships to become manifest, *qi* was necessary. *Qi*, literally "breath" or "air," is often translated as life breath, energy, pneuma, vital essence, material force, primordial substance, psychophysical stuff, and so forth. Unfortunately, no single rendering serves all philosophical and

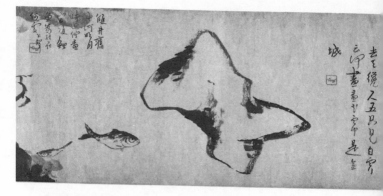

FIGURE 2.1
Detail from Zhu Da's *Fish and Rocks* (Chinese, 1624–1705)
Handscroll; mid- to late 1600s, ink on paper, 29.2 × 157.4 cm.
Copyright The Cleveland Museum of Art. John L. Severance
Fund 1953.247. Reproduced with permission from the Cleveland
Museum of Art.

practical purposes. For now, suffice it to say that in various states of coarseness or refinement, it comprised all objects in the world and filled all the spaces between them. In late Zhou thought, "everything was assumed to be qi in some form, from eminently tangible objects like rocks and logs to more rarefied phenomena like light and heat."[2] Qi was then "simultaneously 'what makes things happen in stuff' and (depending on context) 'stuff that makes things happen' or stuff in which things happen.'"[3]

With respect to human beings, qi in its coarser aspects becomes flesh, blood, and bones, but in its most highly refined manifestation, known as "vital essence," it not only suffuses and animates our bodies but also becomes our "spirit."[4] "Spirit," in late Zhou usage, had a wide range of meanings, as it does in contemporary English. But whereas in English the term almost invariably implies a sharp contrast with the material body, in classical Chinese discourse the distinction was never so clear. Spirit was viewed as an entity within the body that was responsible for consciousness, combining what Westerners would generally distinguish as "heart" and "mind." In other words, the spiritual essence of human beings came to be viewed in terms of "the interface between the sentient and insentient, or the psychological and physical," uniting both aspects rather than insisting on boundaries.[5]

The important point for our purposes is that for well over two thousand years, Chinese of various philosophical persuasions believed that by cultivating their qi to the fullest extent, and thus harnessing the highly refined spiritual capabilities of their minds, they could achieve extraordinary things. Daoist-oriented individuals, for instance, could attain immortality; Confucians, for their part, could literally "transform people" and ultimately change the world by means of ritual rectitude and moral force. According to the *Doctrine of the Mean*, an extremely influential work initially composed in the late Warring States period, the key to Confucian self-cultivation was sincerity—the moral integrity that enables a person to become fully developed as an agent of the cosmos: "Sincerity is Heaven's Way; achieving sincerity is the Way of human beings. One who is sincere attains centrality without striving, apprehends without thinking." The work goes on to assert that the person who possesses the most complete sincerity "is able to give full development to his nature, ... and to the natures of other living things. Being able to give full development to the natures of other living things, he can assist in the transforming and nourishing powers of Heaven and Earth ... [and thus] form a triad with them."[6] In this view, a person with fully developed sincerity can literally know the future and become "like a spirit."

What, then, should such a cultivated individual do? The Confucian answer was to direct one's spirit toward achieving cosmic resonance—that is, a sympathetic vibration of qi across space. This could occur between objects, the way a plucked note on one instrument resonates with the same note on another instrument, but it could also occur in the minds of human beings. In other words resonance, as a theory of "simultaneous, nonlinear causality," was predicated on the idea that like-things could influence like-things on a cosmic as well as a microcosmic scale. Human consciousness was thus "implicit in and susceptible to the same processes of cosmic resonance that [might] affect trees, iron, magnets, and lute strings."[7] In short, harmony prevailed when like-things resonated and unlike-things were in balance.

By the early Han dynasty, these ideas had developed into a systematic philosophy of resonance and correspondence, often described in terms of "correlative thinking." In contrast to Western-style "subordinative thinking," which relates classes of things through substance and emphasizes the idea of "external causation," in Chinese-style correlative thinking "conceptions are not subsumed under one another but placed side by side in a pattern"; things behave in certain ways "not necessarily because of prior actions or [the] impulsions of other things," but because they resonate with other entities and forces in a complex network of associations and correspondences.[8] Applied to cosmology, this sort of correlative thinking encouraged the idea of mutually implicated "force fields" identified, as we shall see, by highly specialized terms and linked with specific numerical values.

Han-style correlative thinking naturally centered heavily on the concepts of yin and yang, which, as indicated above, could accommodate any set of dual coordinates, from abstruse philosophical concepts such as nonbeing and being to such mundane polarities as dark and light. Another important feature of correlative thinking, though somewhat more problematical in the minds of certain scholars, was an emphasis on the so-called five agents (also translated as elements, phases, activities, and so on), identified with the basic qualities or tendencies of earth (stability), metal (sharpness), fire (heat), water (coolness), and wood (growth). Like yin and yang and the eight trigrams, each of the five agents, in various combinations and operating under different temporal and spatial circumstances, had tangible cosmic power embodied in, or exerting influence on, objects of all sorts by virtue of the sympathetic vibration of qi. Whether considered as external forces or intrinsic qualities, yin and yang and the five agents constantly fluctuated and interacted as part of the eternal, cyclical rhythms of nature. Everything depended on timing and the relative strength of the variables involved. By taking into account these variables, one could predict whether movement would be progressive or retrogressive, fast or slow, auspicious or inauspicious.

By the early Han period the five agents had come to be correlated with various seasons, directions, planets, colors, flavors, musical notes, senses, emotions, organs, grains, sacrifices, punishments, and so forth. They were also correlated with different states or phases of yin and yang. As one concrete but relatively simple illustration, let us look at the construction of calendrical time. In terms of yin and yang, the year can be divided into four parts: two solstices and two equinoxes. The winter solstice marks the point of fullest yin, when yang begins to emerge out of the cold. From this point onward, yin starts to decline and yang increases. At the spring equinox, yin and yang are in perfect balance. The process continues until the summer solstice, when yang is at its apex and yin is at its nadir. Thereafter yang declines and yin increases until the winter solstice, when the cycle begins again.

From the standpoint of five agents correlations, during the first month of the lunar calendar the power of wood prevails. This continues until the fourth month, when fire dominates. The sixth month is ruled by earth. The seventh, eighth, and ninth months are controlled by metal, and the tenth, eleventh, and twelfth months fall under the predominant influence of water. Armed with this sort of correlative knowledge, one could determine at any given time of year which directions were most auspicious, which planetary configurations were most favorable, which rituals should be performed, which foods, offerings, and medicines were most appropriate, and so on.[9]

Like yin and yang, the five agents worked in sequences, but the order of displacement indicated above is somewhat unusual, for in the standard "mutual conquest" sequence of the five agents, water conquered fire, fire conquered metal, metal conquered wood, wood conquered earth, and earth conquered water. By contrast, in the "mutual production" sequence, wood produced fire, fire produced earth, earth produced metal, metal produced water, and water produced wood. There have been many explanations of how these two related processes occur in nature, some of which are fairly commonsensical and others of which involve a stretch of the imagination—for instance wood is sometimes said to overcome earth by "digging it" (as with a wooden shovel).

We shall see more of the five agents, along with several related configurations of cosmic power, later in this book. For now the important point to keep in mind is that for the *Changes* to flourish in this particular intellectual environment it needed philosophical flesh, something more substantial and sophisticated than the

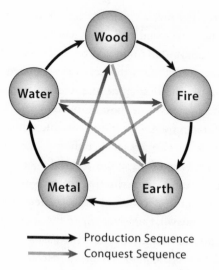

FIGURE 2.2
Five Agents Sequences

bare bones of the basic text. Body weight came in the form of the provocative, sometimes powerful, and often poetic commentaries of the Ten Wings.

The Ten Wings in the Early Life of the *Yijing*

As indicated at the outset of this chapter, the Ten Wings are heterogeneous in content. The first and second wings, together known as the "Commentary on the Judgments," and the third and fourth, collectively titled the "Commentary on the Images," probably date from the sixth or fifth century BCE. They are almost certainly the oldest systematic treatises on the basic text of the *Changes*. The Commentary on the Judgments explains each judgment by referring to its phrases, its hexagram symbolism, or the location of its yin (broken) and yang (solid) lines. The Commentary on the Images consists of two subsections: a "Big-Image Commentary," which discusses the images associated with the two primary trigrams of each hexagram (lines 1–3 and 4–6, respectively), and a "Small-Image Commentary," which refers to the symbolism of the individual lines. The two parts of the "Great Commentary," also known as the "Commentary on the Appended Statements," are generally described as the fifth and sixth wings. Using somewhat different rhetorical devices in each of its two sections, this commentary offers a sophisticated, although sometimes rather disjointed, discussion of both the metaphysics and the morality of the *Changes*, often citing Confucius for authority.

The rest of the Ten Wings lack the divided structure of the first six. The "Commentary on the Words of the Text" addresses only the first two hexagrams of the basic text, and some scholars believe that it represents fragments of a much lengthier but no longer extant work. The "Explaining the Trigrams" commentary consists primarily of correlations that suggest a conscious effort on the part of the author(s) to expand the symbolic repertoire of the *Yijing*. The wing titled "Providing the Sequence of the Hexagrams" aims at justifying the received order of the hexagrams, and the

last, the "Hexagrams in Irregular Order," offers definitions of hexagrams that are often cast in terms of con-
trasting pairs. Different editions of the *Changes* organize this material in different ways.[10]

The Great Commentary is the most philosophically
interesting of the Ten Wings. It probably assumed
something close to its final form around 300 BCE, and
from the Han period to the present this document has
received far more scholarly attention than any other
single wing.[11] We may think of it as an early biography
of the *Changes* in the sense that it attempts to explain
the life and fundamental meaning of the basic text,
using a great many quotations from its line statements
and judgments. The "Appended Statements" commentary of the Mawangdui manuscript performs a similar
function, using much the same language and imagery.

The primary goal of the Great Commentary was to
explain how the hexagrams, trigrams, and lines of the
document duplicated the fundamental processes and
relationships occurring in nature, enabling those who
consult the *Yijing* with sincerity and reverence to par-
take of a potent, illuminating, activating, and transforming spirituality. By participating fully in this spiritual experience, the reader could discern the patterns
of change in the universe and act appropriately. As the
Great Commentary states:

> Looking up, we use it [the *Changes*] to observe the
> configurations of Heaven, and, looking down, we
> use it to examine the patterns of Earth. Thus we

understand the reasons underlying what is hidden and what is clear. We trace things back to their origins then turn back to their ends. Thus we understand the axiom of life and death.... The *Changes* is without consciousness and is without deliberate action. Being utterly still it does not initiate, but when stimulated it is commensurate with all the causes for everything that happens in the world. As such, it has to be the most spiritual thing in the world, for what else could possibly be up to this?[12]

In other words, the *Yijing* showed how human beings could "fill in and pull together the Dao of Heaven and Earth," thus helping to create and maintain cosmic harmony through their spiritual attunement to the patterns and processes of nature. By using the *Changes* responsibly, humans could not only "know fate" but also do something about it.

The process of consulting the *Changes* involved careful contemplation of the "images" associated with, and reflected in, the lines, trigrams, and hexagrams of the basic text. According to the Great Commentary, sages like Fuxi "had the means to perceive the mysteries of the world and, drawing comparisons to them with analogous things, made images out of those things that seemed appropriate."[13] Initially, then, there were only hexagram images, trigram images, and line images—pure signs unmediated by language. But later on, hexagram names, judgments, and line statements appeared in written form to help explain these abstract significa-

tions. Thus subsequent sages came to use words to identify "images of things" (natural phenomena, such as
Heaven and Earth, mountains, rivers, thunder, wind,
and fire), "images of affairs" (social and political phenomena, including institutions, war, famine, marriage,
and divorce), and "images of ideas" (thoughts, mental
pictures, states of mind, emotions, and any other sen-
sory or extrasensory experiences). Later commentators
sometimes likened images to "flowers in the mirror" or
"the moon in the water"—that is, reflections of things
that "cannot be described as either fully present or fully
absent."[14]

Numbers provided an additional tool for understanding patterns of cosmic change. Indeed, the Great
Commentary tells us that in conjunction with hexagrams, numbers "indicate how change and transformation are brought about and how gods and spirits are
activated."[15] Vague but provocative passages such as
these would later inspire an enormous amount of
scholarship designed to identify and explain the complex relationship between "numbers and images," but
the main focus of the Ten Wings is on images. In fact
at certain points in the text this emphasis seems to di-
minish the value of the written word itself. For example the Great Commentary avers that "Writing does
not exhaust words, and words do not exhaust ideas....
The sages [therefore] established images in order to express their ideas exhaustively ... [and] established the
hexagrams in order to treat exhaustively the true innate tendencies of things."[16]

Ideally, then, if one is able to grasp the meaning of the image, words become unnecessary. In fact, however, the ancient sages did their fair share of explicating. For instance the Great Commentary states that "They [the sages] appended phrases to the lines [of the hexagrams] in order to clarify whether they signified good fortune or misfortune and [they] let the hard [yang] and the soft [yin] lines displace each other so that change and transformation could appear." According to this text, good fortune and misfortune involve images of failure or success, respectively. Regret and remorse involve images of sorrow and worry. Change and transformation involve images of advance and withdrawal. It goes on to say:

> The judgments address the images [i.e., the concept of the entire hexagram], and the line texts address the states of change. The terms "auspicious" and "inauspicious" address the failure or success involved. The terms "regret" and "remorse" address the small faults involved. The expression "there is no blame" indicates success at repairing transgressions. . . . The distinction between a tendency either to the petty or to the great is an inherent feature of the hexagrams. The differentiation of good fortune and misfortune depends on the phrases [i.e., the line statements].[17]

The Great Commentary also tells us that the hexagrams "reproduce every action that occurs in the world," and as a result, "once an exemplary person finds himself in a situation, he observes its image and ponders the phrases involved, and, once he takes action, he observes the change [of the lines] and ponders the prognostications involved."[18] Essential to this process was an acute attunement to the seminal first stirrings of change, which afford the opportunity for acting appropriately at the most propitious and efficacious time. The technical term in the *Yijing* for this moment is "incipience" (often described metaphorically as a door hinge, trigger, or pivot)—that "infinitesimally small beginning of action, the point at which the precognition of good fortune can occur."[19] Once again in the words of the Great Commentary, "It is by means of the *Changes* that the sages plumb the utmost profundity and dig into the very incipience of things. It is profundity alone that thus allows one to penetrate the aspirations of all the people in the world; it is a grasp of incipience alone that thus allows one to accomplish the great affairs of the world."[20]

In short, by virtue of their spiritual capabilities and comprehensive symbolism, the sixty-four hexagrams of the *Yijing* provided the means by which to understand all phenomena, including the forces of nature, the interaction of things, and the circumstances of change. Like yin and yang, the five agents, the eight trigrams, and other cosmic variables, hexagrams were always in the process of transformation, but at any given time they also revealed qualities and capacities. These qualities and capacities were naturally reflected in the relationship of the two constituent trigrams within a given hexagram. For instance the Zhen ("Thunder") trigram causes things to move, Sun ("Wind") disperses things, Kan ("Water") moistens things, Li ("Fire") dries things, Gen ("Mountain") causes things to stop, Dui ("Lake") pleases things, Qian ("Heaven") provides governance, and Kun ("Earth") shelters things.[21]

In what other ways did the Ten Wings help to explain the cryptic basic text of the *Changes*? Let us look first at the Commentary on the Judgments and the Commentary on the Images, keeping in mind that the latter commentary provides an analysis of the hexagram imagery as a whole (the "Big Image") as well as an analysis of each individual line (the "Small Image"). The focus here is on the Gen hexagram (number 52), which has already been discussed briefly in both the introduction and chapter 1.

By the early Han dynasty, if not well before, the Zhou dynasty idea that Gen might mean "to cleave" or "to glare at" had given way to a very different conception of the term. From Han times onward, the dominant meanings that came to be attached to the Gen hexagram now had to do with "stillness" and "restraint."[22] Below is a rendering of the basic text of Gen, based on a Han dynasty understanding, together with a few commentaries drawn from the Ten Wings.[23]

Gen

JUDGMENT: Restraint [or Stilling] takes place
with the back, so the person in question does
not obtain the other person. He goes into that

one's courtyard but does not see him there. There is no blame.

COMMENTARY ON THE JUDGMENTS: Gen means "stop." When it is time to stop, one should stop; when it is time to act, one should act. If in one's activity and repose he is not out of step with the times, his Dao should be bright and glorious. Let Restraint operate where restraint should take place, that is, let the restraining be done in its proper place. Those above and those below stand in reciprocal opposition to each other and so do not get along. This is the reason why, although "one does not obtain the other person" and "one goes into one's courtyard but does not see him there," yet there is no blame.

COMMENTARY ON THE IMAGES: United mountains [i.e., doubled Gen trigrams]: this constitutes the image of Restraint. In the same way, the exemplary person is mindful of how he should not go out of his position.

Line 1: Restraint takes place with the toes, so there is no blame, and it is fitting that the person in question practices perpetual perseverance.

COMMENTARY ON THE IMAGES: If "Restraint takes place with the toes," one shall never violate the bounds of rectitude [or "stray off the correct path"].

Line 2: Restraint takes place with the calves, which means that the person in question does not raise up [i.e., rescue] his followers. His heart feels discontent.

COMMENTARY ON THE IMAGES: "The person in question does not raise up his followers," nor does he withdraw and obey the call.

Line 3: Restraint takes place with the midsection, which may split the flesh at the backbone,[24] a danger enough to smoke and suffocate the heart.

COMMENTARY ON THE IMAGES: If "Restraint takes place with the midsection," the danger would "smoke and suffocate the heart."

Line 4: Restraint takes place with the torso. There is no blame.

COMMENTARY ON THE IMAGES: "Restraint takes place with the torso," which means that the person in question applies restraint to his own body.

Line 5: Restraint takes place with the jowls, so the words of the person in question are ordered, and regret vanishes.

COMMENTARY ON THE IMAGES: "Restraint takes place with the jowls," so the person in question is central and correct.

Line 6: The person in question exercises Restraint with simple honesty, which results in good fortune.

COMMENTARY ON THE IMAGES: The good fortune that springs from "exercising Restraint with simple honesty" means that one will reach his proper end because of that simply honesty.

Although these glosses from the Ten Wings certainly did not resolve all ambiguities or eliminate all future controversies regarding the possible meanings of Gen's judgment and line statements,[25] they did underscore a radical interpretive shift that transformed the Gen hexagram from an apparent description of a ritualized sacrifice to a set of prescriptions for self-control and ethical behavior.

In many instances the Commentary on the Judgments focuses not only on the general meaning of the hexagram in question, as indicated in the example above, but also on the specific symbolism of its individual trigrams as well as the meaning of its lines and the relationship between them. For an illustration we may take Tongren (number 13). The Commentary on the Judgments states (in full):

Fellowship is expressed in terms of how a weak line [yin in the second place] obtains a position such that, thanks to its achievement of the Mean, it finds itself in resonance with the [ruler of the] Qian trigram [the yang line in the fifth place]. Such a situation is called Tongren [Fellowship]. When the judgment of the Tongren hexagram says "it is by extending Fellowship even to the fields that one prevails" and "thus it is fitting to cross the great river," it refers to what the Qian trigram accomplishes. Exercising strength through the practice of civility and enlightenment, [the second yin line and the fifth yang line] each respond to the other with their adherence to the Mean and their uprightness: such is the rectitude of the exemplary person. Only the exemplary person would be able to identify with the aspirations of all the people in the world.[26]

The Big-Image Commentary tells us that "This combination of Heaven [the upper trigram, Qian] and Fire [the lower trigram, Li] constitutes the image of Tongren. In the same way the exemplary person associates with his own kind and makes clear distinctions among things."[27]

Although the Big-Image Commentary supplies the overall trigram imagery for each individual hexagram—based, as we have seen, on the relationship of its two primary trigrams—the commentary known as Explaining the Trigrams establishes relationships among all eight. For instance, we are told: "As Heaven [symbolized by the Qian trigram] and Earth [Kun] establish positions, as Mountain [Gen] and Lake [Dui] reciprocally circulate qi, as Thunder [Zhen] and Wind [Sun] give rise to each other, and as Water [Kan] and Fire [Li] unfailingly conquer each other, so the eight trigrams combine with one another in such a way that, to reckon the past, one follows the order of their progress, and, to know the future, one works backward through them."[28] This passage not only indicates that there are important resonant connections among trigrams independent of whatever relationship they might have within any given hexagram; it also indicates that different systems of ordering the trigrams will yield different understandings of the past and the future.

But the Explaining the Trigrams commentary does even more: it attaches meanings to each of the eight trigrams that go well beyond the basic significations they possessed prior to the Han (as indicated in the quotation above and in chapter 1). A careful reading of this commentary reveals, for example, that the trigram Gen not only possesses the fundamental attributes of mountains (restraint, stillness, stopping, stability, endurance); it also has the nature of a dog; it "works like the hand"; it produces the youngest son (as one of the "offspring" of the Qian and Kun trigrams); it signifies maturity; it is located in the northeast; and it has features associated with footpaths, small stones, gate towers, tree fruit, vine fruit, gatekeepers and palace guards, the fingers, rats, the black jaws of birds and beasts of prey, and the attributes of trees that are both sturdy and gnarled.[29]

Similarly, the Sun (also known as Xun) trigram, in addition to its basic meaning of Wind (hence qualities of compliance and accommodation), has the nature of a rooster; it "works like the thigh"; it produces the eldest daughter; it is located in the southeast; and it has features associated with wood; with things that are straight, lengthy, and tall; and with carpenters, freshness, purity, and neatness. We are also told that with respect to men, Sun represents "the balding, the broad in the forehead, the ones with much white in their eyes, the ones who keep close to what is profitable and who market things for threefold gain." At the end point of its development, Sun signifies impetuosity.[30] Let us keep these kinds of trigram associations in mind as we explore the complexities of *Yijing* analysis later on in this biography.

Most of the other Ten Wings say comparatively little about lines or trigrams, although the Great Commentary offers a few general interpretive points to keep in mind. It tells us, for example, that the three odd-numbered (yang) trigrams—Zhen, Kan, and Gen—each of which has one "sovereign" and two "subjects" (i.e., one solid line and two broken lines), show the way of the exemplary person, while the three even-numbered (yin) trigrams—Sun, Li, and Dui—each of which has two "sovereigns" and one "subject" (i.e., two solid lines and one broken line), illustrate the way of the inferior person. The Great Commentary also states that "The first lines [of a hexagram] are difficult to understand, but the top lines are easy, because they are the roots and branches, respectively [i.e., the beginnings and endings]. . . . The second lines [of a hexagram] usually concern honor, while the fourth lines usually concern fear. . . . The third lines usually concern misfortune, while the fifth lines usually concern achievement."[31]

The Providing the Sequence commentary explains the developmental logic of the received order of the hexagrams, but in a rather forced and unconvincing way. It begins:

Only after there were Heaven [Qian, number 1] and Earth [Kun, number 2] were the myriad things produced from them. What fills Heaven and Earth is nothing more than the myriad things. This is why Qian and Kun are followed by Zhun [number 3]. Zhun here signifies repletion. Zhun is when things are first born. When things begin life, they are sure to be covered. This is why Zhun is followed by Meng. Meng [number 4] here indicates juvenile ignorance, that is the immature state of things.[32]

In the Hexagrams in Irregular Order commentary, some of the symbolism is expressly oppositional. Thus, for example, the Qian hexagram (number 1) is represented as hard and firm while Kun (number 2) is described as soft and yielding; Bi (number 8) involves joy while Shi (number 7) indicates dismay. Zhen (number 51) means a start while Gen (number 52) involves a stop. Dui (number 58) means "to show yourself" while Sun (number 57) means "to stay hidden."[33] These interpretations from the Hexagrams in Irregular Order differ significantly from the "demonstrations" and "provisions" laid out in the following passage from the Great Commentary:

Sun ["Compliance," number 57] demonstrates how one can weigh things while yet remaining in obscurity. Lü ["Treading," number 10] provides the means to make one's actions harmonious. Qian ["Modesty," number 15] provides the means by which decorum exercises its control. Fu ["Return," number 24] provides the means to know oneself. Heng ["Perseverance," number 32] provides the means to keep one's virtue whole and intact. Sun ["Diminution," number 41] provides the means to keep harm at a distance. Yi ["Increase," number 42] provides the means to promote benefits. Kun ["Impasse," number 47] provides the means to keep resentments few. Jing ["The Well," number 48] provides the means to distinguish what righteousness really is. Sun ["Compliance," number 57] provides the means to practice improvisations.[34]

Sometimes the Great Commentary organizes hexagrams according to themes, such as the following cluster pertaining to virtue: Lü ("Treading," number 10) "is the foundation of virtue." Qian ("Modesty," number 15) "is how virtue provides a handle on things." Fu ("Return," number 24) "is the root of virtue." Heng ("Perseverance," number 32) "provides virtue with steadfastness." Sun ("Diminution," number 41) "is how virtue is cultivated." Yi ("Increase," number 42) "is how virtue proliferates." Kun ("Impasse," number 47) "is the criterion for distinguishing virtue." Jing ("The Well," number 48) "is the ground from which virtue springs." Sun ("Compliance," number 57) is the controller of virtue.[35]

From the relatively small sample of interpretive possibilities mentioned above, it should be clear that a hexagram like Sun (number 57) might provide several kinds of guidance: (1) how (or why) "to stay hidden," (2) how to weigh things "while yet remaining in obscurity," (3) how to practice improvisations, and (4) how to control virtue. And if we factor the Mawang-dui version of the Sun hexagram into the equation, yet another variable appears: the idea of making "cal-culations" rather than being "compliant."[36] Moreover, as we shall see, the guidelines discussed abosve are only the beginning of *Yijing* consultation. We have not, for example, begun to explore systematically the meaning(s) of Sun's doubled trigrams, their relation-ship with other trigrams (especially Zhen, "Thunder," as indicated above), the developmental structure of Sun's six lines, or the ways that Sun might be related to its "opposite" hexagram, Dui (number 58).

In short, the Ten Wings of the *Yijing*, even without the alternative readings provided by the Mawangdui manuscript and other versions of the *Changes*, vastly enhanced its symbolic repertoire. Although the con-tent of the classic became fixed in 136 BCE, for the next two thousand years scholars and diviners enjoyed an enormous amount of latitude in interpreting the work. In the meantime the Great Commentary be-came the locus classicus for virtually all discussions in China of time, space, and metaphysics, investing the *Yijing* with extraordinary philosophical authority. In addition this amplified and state-sanctioned version of the *Changes* became a repository of concrete symbols and general explanations that proved serviceable in such diverse realms of knowledge as art, literature, music, mathematics, science, and medicine.

Interpreting the *Changes*

CHAPTER 3

Approaches to the *Yijing*—whether scholarly or divinatory—have naturally hinged on factors such as philosophical or religious affiliations, intellectual fashions, politics, social status, gender, personal taste, family ties, and other variables of time, place, and circumstance. As Chinese society evolved, new ways of thinking about the classic arose, inexorably expanding the scope of interpretive possibilities to include virtually every emerging realm of knowledge. Thus, over the course of more than two millennia, thousands of commentaries were written on the *Changes*, each amplifying the text and each reflecting a distinctive technical, philological, religious, philosophical, literary, social, or political point of view. Not surprisingly, then, the document came to be identified by some Chinese scholars as a "mirror of history" as well as a "mirror of the human mind." Although I have separated discussions of the scholarly and the divinatory uses of the *Yijing* in this chapter, it should be obvious that they have always been closely connected.[1]

Commentarial Traditions in Early Imperial China (136 BCE–960 CE)

Different schools of *Yijing* interpretation developed almost immediately after the work had attained classic status in 136 BCE. As indicated in the previous chapter, at least some of these schools had their origins during the late Warring States period, when different versions of the *Changes* began to circulate. The Han dynasty (206 BCE–220 CE) was a critical period in the history of Chinese philosophy generally, and *Yijing* interpretation in particular, but very few complete or authentic works relating to the *Changes* actually date from that time. Thus until recently most of what we knew about Han approaches to the *Yijing* had been derived from secondary sources and fragments of Han texts preserved in encyclopedias, literary anthologies, and other such collections.

One fundamental division that emerged during the Han period was between the so-called New Text and Old Text schools of classical scholarship, distinctions based on different versions and different understandings of the Confucian classics that surfaced after the Qin dynasty's infamous burning of the books in 213 BCE. In brief, New Text scholars tended to deify Confucius, stress commonalities between the emperor and all other people, and employ a broad range of written materials—including numerically oriented predictive charts and formulas of the so-called Apocrypha—to defend their positions. Old Text scholars, by contrast, viewed Confucius as simply a sage, exalted the sovereign over both officials and commoners, and adopted a more rationalistic and critical attitude toward both the classics and the Apocrypha.[2]

The state considered New Text interpretations orthodox during most of the Early or Western Han period (up to 9 CE). But following the usurpation of Wang Mang (r. 9–23), versions of the classics written in a more archaic form began to appear, and during the Later or Eastern Han period (23–220), these editions, and the interpretive traditions that accompanied them, came to be seen as orthodox. For the next fifteen hundred years or so, Old Text Confucianism dominated Chinese intellectual life, but, as we shall see, New Text–style numerology never died.

New Text scholars of the early Han period sought, among other things, to identify correspondences between the various features of the natural world (both physical and metaphysical) and the hexagrams, trigrams, and individual lines of the *Changes*. These correspondences often involved numerical correlations because—as with the Pythagoreans in ancient Greece—numbers provided cosmologically inclined individuals with a systematic explanation of the universe and its movements. They provided a way of domesticating nature, of submitting it to the premodern equivalent of equations. From a practical standpoint, an understanding of numbers enabled human beings to determine how best to situate themselves in a harmonious relationship with their environment.

According to the Great Commentary, when numbers are combined in various ways, they "exhaust all aspects of change"; thus a mastery of numbers enables one to "know the future."[3] For this reason a significant amount of this commentary is devoted to various numerological discussions. For instance we are told that the numbers of Heaven are one, three, five, seven, and nine (all yang numbers) and the numbers of Earth are two, four, six, eight, and ten (all yin numbers). The sum of the five Heavenly numbers is twenty-five, and the sum of the five Earthly numbers is thirty; together they come to fifty-five.[4] The Great Commentary also describes in detail a method for divining with fifty milfoil stalks that involves dividing the stalks into numerical groups that symbolize yin and yang (two); Heaven, Earth, and Humanity (three); and the seasons (four).[5] It is easy enough to imagine how these numbers, both alone and in combination, came to be correlated with all kinds of phenomena, from musical notes and heavenly bodies to divisions of time and space.[6] Such correlations revealed cosmic connections—spiritual resonances that existed between like things. As such they explained how the universe operated and, more important, how it might be manipulated.

New Text scholarship marked the beginning of what would become known as the School of Images and Numbers, in contrast to the School of Meanings and Principles. The former school emphasized mathematical calculations and correlations of the sort described above; the latter was more closely associated with Old Text sources, and its exponents paid primary attention to what they saw as the moral content of the judgments, line statements, and commentaries to the *Changes*.

One of the most influential early interpreters of the *Yijing* was Jing Fang (77–37 BCE). Known primarily as a divination specialist but also identified as an exponent of New Text scholarship and an advocate of the Images and Numbers approach to the *Changes*,[7] he has been credited with inventing or popularizing several calendrically based schemes for linking phases of change with markers of time. These systems involved correlations among a wide range of cosmic variables, including yin and yang, the five agents, the eight trigrams, the sixty-four hexagrams, and units of space and time such as the ten heavenly stems and twelve earthly branches (operating either individually or in combination), the twenty-four segments of the solar year, and the twenty-eight lunar lodges (see figure 3.1).[8]

The elaborate details of these systems need not concern us here.[9] The important point is that they all attempted to provide ways of identifying cosmically ordained and numerically accessible patterns of cyclical change so that human beings could select auspicious times and places for various activities, from solemn, state-sponsored rituals to the most mundane personal affairs. This was also the purpose of Jing Fang's relatively simple depiction of twelve "waxing and waning" hexagrams, whose respective broken and solid lines

FIGURE 3.1

Correlations among the Trigrams, Hexagrams, and Twenty-Four
Segments of the Solar Year, attributed to Jing Fang.

In this Qing dynasty chart, the trigrams Kan, Zhen, Li, and Dui,
located in the innermost circle, are correlated with the four
compass points and the four seasons. The twenty-four lines of
these four trigrams are correlated with the twenty-four calendrical
divisions of the 360-day year (the second ring from the middle),
each of which is 15 days in length. The calendar year, in turn, is
divided into sixty parts. Each of these is marked by a hexagram
that symbolizes the "natural" activity of that period as well as an
"official" position. Thus, for instance, during the beginning of the
first month, marked by the onset of spring and dominated by the
Kan trigram, the Xiaoguo hexagram (number 62 in the received
sequence), representing the first subdivision of this period, is
linked with the official title of "marquis" and the natural activity
of easterly winds dissipating the cold.

suggested an annual cycle of rising and falling, marked by six hexagrams with increasing numbers of yang lines culminating in Qian (number 1), followed by six hexagrams with increasing numbers of yin lines, culminating in Kun (number 2).[10] Here are the waxing hexagrams:

24	19	11	34	43	1
Fu	Lin	Tai	Dazhuang	Kuai	Qian

Jing Fang is also famous for developing several interpretive devices that have remained influential in the analysis of the *Yijing* up to the present day. One of these is the idea of "matching positions" (also known as "correct positions"); another is the notion of "nuclear trigrams" (also known as "interlocking" or "overlapping" trigrams").[11]

Matching positions refers to yang (solid, odd-numbered) lines that occupy odd-numbered places in a hexagram and yin (broken, even-numbered) lines that rest in even-numbered places. Only one hexagram, Jiji ("Ferrying Complete," number 63), has matching lines in all six positions, and only one, Weiji ("Ferrying Incomplete," number 64), has no matching lines at all (see below). Because all its lines are in their "correct" positions, the Jiji hexagram is generally viewed as highly favorable and indicative of stability, cultural development, and personal refinement. Nonetheless, the Commentary on the Judgments warns that although the yang and yin lines of the hexagram "behave correctly," if one ceases to practice constancy and no longer follows a "middle path," chaos will ensue.[12]

Jiji   Weiji

By the same token, although the judgment of Weiji states that "There is nothing at all fitting here," the Commentary on the Judgments indicates that even if the yin and yang lines are not in the correct positions, "the hard and strong and the soft and weak all form resonant relationships," and so "ferrying" (progress) is still possible.[13]

What are "resonant relationships?" They occur when opposite lines occupy analogous yin and yang positions in the lower ("inner") and upper ("outer") primary trigrams (lines 1–3 and 4–6, respectively). That is, the first line of the lower trigram, whether yin or yang, resonates with its opposite in the first line of the upper trigram (line 4 of the hexagram as a whole). In the same way, opposite lines in the second and fifth lines resonate, as do opposite lines in the third and sixth positions. Such oppositions are generally most propitious when the lines occupy their correct positions in the hexagram, but, as we have seen, this was extremely rare for all six lines. In any case the most important resonant lines in a given hexagram tend to be those that occupy the second and fifth places, which represent, respectively, the proper relationship between the official and the ruler, the son and the father, and the wife and the husband.[14]

The nuclear trigram approach to the *Changes* proved to be an especially useful device for opening up interpretive possibilities. It was based on the idea that every hexagram has, in addition to its two primary trigrams (lines 1–3 and 4–6, respectively), two overlapping trigrams (lines 2–4 and 3–5, respectively). These nuclear trigrams, in combination, yield another related hexagram, which generally requires consultation.[15]

In the case of Jiji ("Ferrying Complete"), as we have just seen, the primary trigrams are Li ("Fire") below and Kan ("Water") above. This trigram symbolism indicates, at the most rudimentary level, the idea of a congenial balance of elements (for instance water in a kettle being heated by a flame)—which is also the positive connotation of the Jiji hexagram as a whole. By contrast, although the nuclear trigrams of Jiji are the same as the primary trigrams (Li and Kan), their positions are reversed (with Kan at the bottom and Li on top), suggesting the notion of imbalance (as, for example, when water in a kettle boils over and extinguishes the flame). The hexagram produced by these two nuclear trigrams is Weiji ("Ferrying Incomplete"), for which the Commentary on the Images explicitly counsels the need for the exemplary person to put things in proper order.[16]

Later Han scholars, such as Zheng Xuan (127–200 CE), Xun Shuang (128–190), and Yu Fan (164–233), embraced most of the New Text ideas discussed above.[17] But they also made their own distinctive contributions to the already substantial interpretive repertoire of the *Changes*. Zheng, for example, developed a way of analyzing the individual lines of a hexagram in such a fashion that they could refer to trigrams that were not actually present in the hexagram(s) under consideration.[18] Zheng's name has also been closely associated with a number of *Yijing*-related apocryphal texts that employ calendrical and numerological methods for predictive purposes. One of these, *Opening Up the Regularities of Qian*, reads like a sophisticated tract on the Great Commentary itself.[19]

Xun Shuang is best known for his theory of ascending and descending lines and trigrams, which came to be closely linked to the idea that the six lines of a hexagram can represent different levels of social or bureaucratic status as well as the developmental stages of a situation (see below).[20] Viewed hierarchically rather than developmentally, and by family analogy (as discussed briefly above), line 5 might represent the husband and line 2 the wife. The line statements would then pertain to these relationships, and once again the interpretive possibilities were virtually endless.[21]

> Line 6: The Sage
> Line 5: The Ruler
> Line 4: The Minister
> Line 3: Middle-Ranking Official
> Line 2: Lower Official
> Line 1: Commoner

Yu Fan's interpretive claim to fame was his emphasis on "lost images," "laterally linked hexagrams," and "changing positions." Lost images refers to trigram qualities that go well beyond the already ample symbolism provided by the Explaining the Trigrams wing of the *Yijing* discussed in chapter 2.[22] Over time these lost images came to number in the hundreds. For instance, a list appended to a nineteenth-century Chinese work titled *Historical Mirror of Changes Studies* identifies sixty-six different qualities associated with the Qian trigram alone, including types of people (the king, the sage, the exemplary person, the military man, the traveler, etc.), values (reverence, faithfulness, knowledge, virtue, love, etc.), and general attributes or activities (goodness, greatness, blessings, abundance, benefits, purity, order, height, maturity, awesomeness, severity, anger, beginning, etc.).

The notion of laterally linked hexagrams has to do with the way a new hexagram can be produced from an original one by changing each line of the first from yin to yang or yang to yin. Changing positions refers to a similar practice, but one in which not all the lines of a hexagram are transformed into their opposites.[23]

Taken together, this vast arsenal of interpretive techniques made it possible for Han and later scholars to invest a given hexagram or combination of hexagrams with virtually any meaning. Let us take as an admittedly extreme example Yu Fan's gloss on the top line statement of Lü ("The Wanderer," number 56), which reads: "This bird gets its nest burnt. The Wanderer first laughs and later howls and wails. He loses his ox in a time of ease, which means misfortune." This is how Yu explains the relationship between this line statement, the structure of the hexagram, and the line statement of a derivative hexagram:

> The trigram Li is a bird and is fire; the trigram Sun is wood and is high. The fourth line loses its position, changing into the trigram Zhen, which is a basket, the image of a nest. Now, the image of a nest is not apparent; therefore the bird burns its nest. The trigram Zhen refers to laughing, and . . . [it also signifies the idea of] a beginning, and thus we have laughing at the outset. The response is in the trigram Sun. Sun signifies howling and wailing, and the image of Sun [signifies the idea of] afterward; thus howling and wailing take place later. When the third line moves [changes to a yin line], the trigram Kun is an ox, and when the fifth line moves [changes to a yang line], it forms the trigram Qian, and Qian is ease. The top line loses the third line. The fifth line moves in response to the second line, thus the ox is lost in time of ease. Losing its position and being without a response, it is therefore inauspicious. If the fifth line changes, it forms the hexagram Dun ["Withdrawal," number 33], the second line [of which refers to the idea of] "holding with yellow ox hide"—the lost ox of the traveler's family.[24]

Although all this complex trigram symbolism can be traced to the techniques described above, the precise reasons that the lines change and "lose their position" in this particular instance are never made clear. Small wonder, then, that a great many Chinese scholars, both past and present, have criticized the "excesses" of this radically complex approach to Images and Numbers in the *Changes*.

One of the most vociferous early critics of Images and Numbers scholarship was Wang Bi (226–49), the progenitor of what became known as Abstruse Learning, a creative amalgamation of both Confucian and Daoist thought.[25] Wang rejected the interpretations of Han thinkers like Zheng Xuan, Xun Shuang, and Yu Fan almost entirely in favor of a Meanings and Principles approach to the *Yijing* that stripped away virtually all the complex and often confusing numerical, astrological, and calendrical calculations that Jing Fang and his successors had attached to the work.[26]

The term "image" meant something very different to Wang Bi from what it did to his late Han predecessors. Rather than viewing a hexagram or trigram image as something that could be quantified, calibrated, or extended metaphorically with seemingly infinite specificity and complexity, Wang considered hexagrams and trigrams to be a more general means of understanding processes of change. Whereas Later Han commentators like Zheng, Xun, and Yu measured the meaning and value of a hexagram in terms of its relationship to other hexagrams, all of which were enmeshed in an elaborate web of numerological and other symbolic correspondences, Wang Bi focused on individual hexagrams and the way they illuminated changing situations. As Wang put the matter in his famous essay "General Remarks on the *Zhou Changes*": "When we cite the name of a hexagram, in its meaning we find the controlling principle, and when we read the words of the judgment, then we have got more than half the ideas involved. . . . The hexagrams deal with moments of time and the lines are concerned with the states of change that are appropriate to those times."[27]

Thus in virtually all his commentaries on individual hexagrams, Wang takes pains to spell out the nature of every line and its relationship with other lines or trigrams. For him each hexagram, whether auspicious or inauspicious, simple or complicated, symbolizes the possibility of change. "First, a hexagram denotes a specific situation (or *shi*), such as war, peace, harmony, discord, conflict, and reconciliation. Second, the six lines of a hexagram represent the room to maneuver within that particular situation (or *yong*), showing both the hidden dangers and the available options." At this precise juncture, between what is "fated" and what can be done, Wang Bi emphasizes "the fluidity of human affairs and the importance of making the right decision."[28]

The only major interpretive principles that Wang shared with commentators from the Late Han period were (1) the view that certain hexagram lines can resonate productively with one another, and (2) the notion that the lines can represent—either directly or by analogy—different kinds of people in different positions and social situations. Under most circumstances, however, Wang chose to emphasize the temporal and developmental significance of the individual lines within the framework of a single hexagram. In his words: "Moments of time entail either obstruction or facility, thus the application [of a given hexagram] is a matter either of action or of withdrawal."

Once the critical ("incipient") moment of time has been determined, "one should either act or remain passive, responding to the type of application involved." One contemplates the name of the hexagram in order to see whether the general situation portends good fortune or bad, and one cites what is said about the incipient moment in order to see whether one should act or remain passive. From these indicators, "it is apparent how change operates within the body of one hexagram."[29] So, for instance, in glossing the Gen hexagram ("Restraint," number 52), which I have referred to previously on several occasions and will refer to again, Wang points out that the third yang line portends danger, indicating the need for great caution and care, because of its position at the "backbone" of the hexagram (i.e., its location between a pair of yin lines on either side).

Gen

By the end of the Six Dynasties period (220–589 CE), Wang Bi's commentary on the *Changes*, amplified by the remarks of Han Kangbo (ca. 332–385?), had gained ascendancy among scholars of the *Yijing*.[30] This ascendancy continued into the Sui (589–618) and Tang (618–907) dynasties, especially after Wang's edition of the text became the centerpiece of Kong Ying-da's (574–648) *Correct Meaning of the Zhou Changes*, which remained the official version of the *Yijing* throughout the Tang and into the Song (907–1279) and Yuan (1279–1368) dynasties.

Han-style New Text scholarship and Images and Numbers interpretations did not disappear entirely, however. In fact, in some circles there was a resurgence of Han-style correlative thinking. During the Tang period, for example, the five agents were first matched systematically with the eight trigrams.[31] In the most common configuration, the Qian and Dui trigrams shared the agent metal; Sun and Zhen shared wood, and Gen and Kun shared earth. Kan was linked solely with water, and Li was associated only with fire (see figure 3.2). As with all other correlative cosmologies, the goal was to assure that in any given situation the conjunction of symbolic elements—whether trigrams, agents, or numbers—would be harmonious and therefore auspicious. But to critics of this sort of cosmological thinking, like the Tang scholar Lü Cai (600–664) and his successors, efforts to correlate incommensurate numbers represented nothing more than a forced fit.

It was during the Tang dynasty that Buddhist and Daoist ideas, which had already begun to influence *Yijing* scholarship in the Six Dynasties period, gained ever greater visibility. Proponents of Daoist alchemy,

FIGURE 3.2
Trigram and Five Agents Correlations
In this Qing dynasty diagram, the eight trigrams occupy the outer
ring, with the five agents located directly below each named
trigram. Some agents are duplicated. Patterns of production and
conquest are indicated by lines and written characters.

for instance, in their quest for longevity and eventual
immortality, increasingly saw the *Changes* as a convenient device by which to align the body and mind with
the cosmos. Thus the Tang period witnessed the first
major commentaries on the Daoist work titled *Token
for the Agreement of the Three According to the Zhou
Changes*—perhaps the most famous and influential of
all Chinese alchemical texts. This tract "fully exploited

the imagery of the *Book of Changes*, and incorporated other established cosmological correlations and symbols, not only for alchemical process but . . . [also to illustrate] the relations of multiplicity and change with 'the unity and the constancy of the Dao.'"[32]

Likewise Tang Buddhists, building on Six Dynasty precedents, engaged the *Yijing* to an unprecedented extent. The *Changes*-related writings of individuals such as Li Tongxuan (635–730), Yixing (638–727?), Chengguan (738–839?), Zongmi (780–841), Dongshan Liangjie (807–69), and Caoshan Benji (840–901) show how Buddhism—particularly the variety known as Flowery Splendor—interacted with the *Yijing*, not only borrowing concepts from the classic but also enriching it by expanding the range of its interpretive possibilities.[33] From this point onward, Buddhist terminology, imagery, and symbolism increasingly found their way into the analysis of the *Changes*.

Interpretations of the *Changes* in Late Imperial and Postimperial Times (960 CE–Present)

The intellectual and institutional challenges posed by Buddhism in the Tang dynasty resulted in the rise of Neo-Confucianism during the Song dynasty. This new brand of metaphysically oriented Confucianism drew heavily on the *Yijing* as a domestic source of inspiration, a counterweight to the "alien" ideas of Buddhism. Neo-Confucianism took two major forms in the Song

CHAPTER 3

period and thereafter. One was the so-called School of Principle, which focused on the idea that in order to cultivate the "principle" (a kind of "Platonic ideal") of one's innate goodness, it was necessary to study the Confucian classics assiduously, thus refining one's qi from without, so to speak. The other was the so-called School of the Mind, which emphasized the value of seeking the principle of the innately good self within, primarily through meditation. Both schools placed a heavy emphasis on the power of the mind, however. Thus, for all his insistence on the importance of book-learning, one of the leading exponents of the School of Principle, Cheng Yi (1033–1107), could write that, "With the most highly developed sincerity, [the mind] can penetrate metal and stone, and overcome water and fire, so what dangers and difficulties can possibly keep it from prevailing?"[34]

During the Song period, for the first time in Chinese history, the *Changes* received more scholarly attention than any other Confucian classic, and it would continue to do so for the remainder of the imperial era. One of the many noteworthy features of early Song scholarship on the *Yijing* is the profusion of charts and diagrams that suddenly appeared at that time, many of which have been attributed to a Daoist master named Chen Tuan (871–989).[35] These illustrations, although usually associated with the School of Images and Numbers, came to be attached to the writings of many Song and later scholars commonly identified with the School of Meanings and Principle—one of many indi-

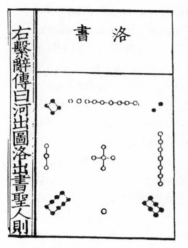
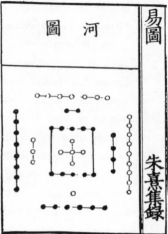

FIGURE 3.3
The Lo River Writing (*left*) and the Yellow River Chart (*right*)
Both illustrations are from a Song dynasty book on the *Yijing*.

cations of the limits of these and other such evaluative categories in the history of *Changes* scholarship.

The most influential of these early diagrams were the "Yellow River Chart," the "Luo River Writing," the "Former Heaven Chart," and the "Later Heaven Chart" (see figures 3.3 and 3.4).[36] All four came to be seen as maps of the cosmos, symbolic guides to its inner workings and outward manifestations.

The Yellow River Chart arranges the numbers from one to ten in such a way as to pair odd (yang) numbers with even (yin) ones. These numbers are then correlated with the five directions (and hence the five agents): two and seven to the south (fire), one and six to the north (water), three and eight to the east (wood), four and nine to the west (metal), and five and ten at the center (earth). As we saw in chapter 2, in the "mutual production" sequence of the five agents, wood produces fire, fire produces earth, earth produces metal, metal produces water, and water produces wood. In the "mutual conquest" sequence, water conquers fire, fire conquers metal, metal conquers wood, wood conquers earth, and earth conquers water. In the Yellow River Chart, which reflects the mutual production sequence of the five agents, all the odd

FIGURE 3.4

The Later Heaven (*left*) and Former Heaven (*right*) Sequences
Both illustrations are from a Qing dynasty book on the *Yijing*.

numbers add up to twenty-five, and all the even numbers add up to thirty.[37]

In the Luo River Writing we find a "magic square," in which the numbers in any row of three, whether perpendicular, horizontal, or diagonal, add up to fifteen. Even (yin) numbers occupy all four corners, and the five agents sequence is one of mutual conquest. Thus, for example, wood (three and eight) overcomes earth (five and ten), earth overcomes water (one and six), water overcomes fire (two and seven), fire overcomes metal (four and nine), and metal overcomes wood.[38]

The Former Heaven Chart, attributed to Fuxi, displays the eight trigrams in four sets, each corresponding to one of the four seasons (usually depicted in clockwise order, with summer located in the south, at the top of the diagram). The juxtapositions in this configuration are Qian (south) and Kun (north); Sun (southwest) and Zhen (northeast); Kan (west) and Li (east); and Gen (northwest) and Dui (southeast). According to the Explaining the Trigrams commentary, the clockwise movement of the trigrams from Zhen through Li and Dui to Qian takes into account what is already existing while the counterclockwise movement of the trigrams from Sun through Kan and Gen to Kun takes into account what has not yet come into existence. In terms of their direct "effects in nature," as discussed briefly in chapter 2, Zhen ("Thunder") causes things to move, Sun ("Wind") disperses things, Kan ("Water") moistens things, Li ("Fire") dries things, Gen ("Mountain") causes things to stop, Dui ("Lake") pleases things, Qian ("Heaven") provides governance, and Kun ("Earth") shelters things.[39]

The Later Heaven Chart, attributed to King Wen, presents the trigrams in a spatial order that depicts yet another kind of developmental change. In the most common version of this scheme, Zhen (east) marks the beginning of the Later Heaven cycle, followed by Sun (southeast), Li (south), Kun (southwest), Dui (west), Qian (northwest), Kan (north), and Gen (northeast). In this sequence all things come forth in Zhen ("Thunder"), they are set in order in Sun ("Wind"), they are made visible to one another in Li ("Fire"), they are nourished by Kun ("Earth"), they are pleased by Dui ("Lake"), they contend in Qian ("Heaven"), they toil in Kan ("Water"), and they reach maturity in Gen ("Mountain").[40]

Not surprisingly the four illustrations discussed above became mutually implicated. Thus, for instance, the Luo River Writing came to be paired with the Former Heaven Chart (figure 3.5), and the Yellow River Chart came to be paired with both the Former and the Later Heaven Chart. Over time the cosmological relationships became increasingly complex.[41] Figure 3.6 shows, for example, correlations among the decimal number system of the Yellow River Chart, the eight trigrams, the five agents, and the ten heavenly stems in various configurations. In each case the purpose of the correlations was to create a comprehensive vision of reality, one in which number and image, as well as past, present, and future, were seamlessly integrated.

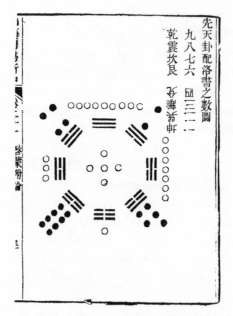

FIGURE 3.5
The Luo River Writing and the Former Heaven Sequence
From a Qing dynasty book on the *Yijing*.

Naturally the wide variety of formulations invited a great deal of criticism from different angles,[42] but the effort to build comprehensive models continued unceasingly.

One of the great Images and Numbers systems builders of the Song period was Shao Yong (1011–77), whose book *Supreme Principles That Rule the World* received praise for its comprehensiveness as well as criticism for its effort to "force" some of its correlations and for taking liberties with the conventional

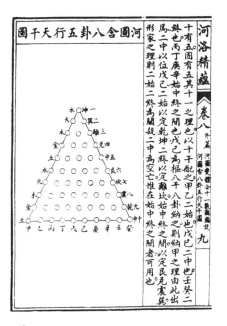

FIGURE 3.6

Triangular Diagram of Yellow River Chart Correlations
In this Qing dynasty diagram, the right side of the triangle,
displaying the numbers 1–10 (with 1 at the top), has four trigrams
corresponding to 1–4 and four trigrams corresponding to 6–9.
The numbers 5 and 10 on this side represent the middle of the
Yellow River Chart (see figure 3.3). On the left side of the triangle,
the five agents are represented twice in neither the production
nor the conquest order. At the bottom are the ten heavenly stems,
depicted in their conventional order from left to right. In order to
correlate the ten stems with the eight trigrams, the Qian trigram
is linked with the yang stems named Jia (1) and Ren (9) and the
Kun trigram is linked with the yin stems designated Yi (2) and
Gui (10). The interactions of these cosmic variables are symbolized by the small circles of the triangle, which represent the
twenty-five Heavenly numbers and the thirty Earthly numbers of
the Yellow River Chart.

symbolism of the *Changes*. We shall hear more of him in chapters 4 and 5. For Shao, as for virtually all other Neo-Confucians in late imperial China, the source of all cosmic movement was the "Supreme Ultimate," a concept derived from a brief reference in the Great Commentary. The Supreme Ultimate came to be identified as the eternal generative force that produced all things, equivalent to both Heaven and the Dao. In Shao's view it produced numbers, numbers yielded images, and images became concrete objects, all composed of qi.[43]

Shao believed that the eight trigrams were the basic elements of which all things were ultimately constituted. They were engendered by the interaction of yin and yang, which produced four two-line images (sometimes known as "digrams"), representing (1) greater yin (two broken lines, correlated with the Dui trigram), (2) lesser yin (a broken line resting above a solid line, correlated with the Zhen trigram), (3) greater yang (two solid lines, correlated with the Qian trigram), and (4) lesser yang (a solid line resting above a broken line, correlated with the Li trigram). These four images, in turn, were related to four images designated "greater weakness" (correlated with the Kun trigram), "lesser weakness" (correlated with the Kan trigram), "greater strength" (correlated with the Gen trigram), and "lesser strength" (correlated with the Sun trigram).[44]

From these two sets of images other sets followed: four celestial images (sun, moon, stars, and zodiacal space), four terrestrial images (water, fire, soil, and

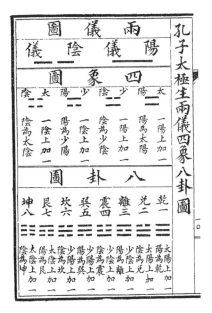

FIGURE 3.7
Production of the Eight Trigrams from the Supreme Ultimate
Reading each line in this Qing dynasty chart horizontally from
right to left, we see that the two poles (yang and yin) of the
Supreme Ultimate generate the four images (greater yang, lesser
yin, lesser yang, and greater yin), which in turn differentiate into
the eight trigrams, beginning with Qian and ending with Kun.

stone), and a host of other "natural" groupings of
four—seasons, directions, limbs, virtues, stages of life,
sense organs, and so forth.[45] Some of these groupings
may not seem so natural, however. The Gen trigram,
for example, representing "greater strength," came to
be correlated with a four-part category consisting of
(1) odors and fire, (2) daytime and wind, (3) the *Classic*

of Poetry and flying things, and (4) the stomach and bone marrow. Shao also developed a vast system of numerical correspondences, based in part on the numbers associated with the Yellow River Chart, to "more precisely define the relationship of things, predict the future, and comprehend vast quantities of space and time."[46] In Shao's complex system of reckoning, numbers in one sequence described aspects of the present or the past, and in a different sequence they revealed the future.[47]

Scholars of the School of Principle such as Cheng Yi resisted this sort of numerological system building. For them the *Yijing* was above all a moral document, to be used solely for cultivating sageliness within and then manifesting it in service to society.[48] In his highly influential commentaries, Cheng steadfastly refused to see the *Changes* as anything more than a text encouraging right behavior, although in his private conversations he was somewhat ambivalent about the numerology of scholars such as Shao Yong.

Zhu Xi (1130–1200), a towering figure in traditional Chinese thought,[49] tried to negotiate a path to understanding the *Yijing* that would avoid the moralistic extremes of Cheng Yi as well as the numerological excesses of Shao Yong, feeling that "Confucians who talk about images and numbers give strained interpretations and draw far-fetched analogies, while those who preach [only] meanings and principles stray far from the subject."[50] Fundamentally Zhu considered the *Changes* to be a book of divination. "What is described in it," he wrote, "is simply images and numbers by which to foretell one's good or evil fortune."[51] But he also believed that the ultimate purpose of the *Yijing* was self-cultivation, and that without sincerity and the rectification of character the work would be of no use as a divinatory device. Zhu's understanding of the classic was thus fundamentally within the framework of the School of Principle. Indeed this branch of learning would later be identified as the Cheng-Zhu School, a combination of the family names of Cheng Yi and Zhu Xi.[52]

Because of his interest in divination, Zhu Xi was more open than some of his colleagues to the ideas of Han thinkers such as Jing Fang and Song system builders such as Shao Yong. For example he used Jing's so-called Eight Palaces system to explain how the eight trigrams changed systematically into the sixty-four hexagrams,[53] and he often cited Shao in explaining the profound cosmological significance of the Yellow River Chart and the Luo River Writing. In fact he was so taken by these two newly "discovered" illustrations that he incorporated them directly into his *Introduction to Changes Studies* and his *Fundamental Meaning of the Zhou Changes*, arguing that the culture hero Fuxi had drawn on the numerology of these two diagrams long ago in laying the foundations of the *Yijing*. For centuries this move engendered much controversy, not only in China but also in other parts of East Asia.

Despite such controversy, Zhu Xi's understanding of the *Changes* became state orthodoxy for much of the Yuan dynasty (1279–1368) and for virtually all of the Ming (1368–1644) and Qing (1644–1912) dynasties; thus his opinions on the classic were powerfully reinforced by the civil service examination system. Nonetheless, as had been the case with the state's sponsorship of Wang Bi's interpretations during the Tang and Song periods, Zhu's views did not go unchallenged. Although many scholars naturally followed the School of Principle, some did not. One such individual, Yang Jian (1141–1226), who approached the *Changes* from the standpoint of the School of the Mind, was so hostile to the ideas of Cheng Yi and Zhu Xi that he reportedly avoided entirely the term "principle" in his writings.

Overall most Chinese scholars tended to be eclectic. Thus the boundaries between the School of Principle and the School of the Mind, like those between the School of Meanings and Principles and the School of Images and Numbers, proved to be quite permeable in practice. Great *Yijing* systems builders, notably Lai Zhide (1525–1604), drew from many different sources of intellectual inspiration, including not only Jing Fang in the Han and Shao Yong and Zhu Xi in the Song, but also certain Buddhist thinkers. Scholars such as Lin Zhaoen (1517–98) and Jiao Hong (ca. 1540–1620) displayed a similar eclecticism in the Ming dynasty. In the Qing period, scientifically minded individuals such as Fang Yizhi (1611–71) and Jiang Yong (1681–1762) incorporated Western mathematical and astronomical ideas, as well as a profound understanding of the *Changes*, into their creative and multifaceted scholarship.

Even devoutly Buddhist scholars like Ouyi Zhixu (1599–1655) drew freely from Confucian and other writings. The preface to Zhixu's *A Chan [Zen] Interpretation of the Zhou Changes* indicates that his purpose in explicating the *Yijing* is "to introduce Chan Buddhism into Confucianism in order to entice Confucians to know Chan."[54] Somewhat ironically his commentary seems more Confucian than Buddhist, and his Buddhist remarks often seem like afterthoughts, with no clear connection to the text of the *Yijing* itself. In the end, like a true Buddhist, Zhixu sought to erase distinctions rather than to reconcile them. The Daoist cleric Liu Yiming (1724–1831), on the other hand, sought to bring Confucianism and Daoism together by arguing that Daoist ideas of mental and alchemical refinement were perfectly compatible with Confucian notions of moral self-cultivation. Indeed, according to Liu's book, *Elucidating the Truth of the Zhou Changes*, the Way of the Confucian sages was the same as the Way of the Daoist immortals.[55]

The Qing dynasty witnessed the rise to prominence of a new kind of scholarship known as Evidential Studies, which sought to rid the Confucian classics, including the *Yijing*, of course, of Buddhist and Daoist accretions, which scholars of this intellectual persuasion blamed on the rise of Song Neo-Confucianism. Using sophisticated philological techniques to expose interpolations and other distortions in both "original" texts and later commentaries, exponents of this school generally looked to Han dynasty materials for inspiration rather than to Song dynasty sources, on the grounds that the Han sources were closer to the time of Confucius and essentially free from corrosive Buddhist and Religious Daoist influences. Predictably most of these scholars castigated Zhu Xi for attaching the Yellow River Chart and the Luo River Writing to his "orthodox" writings on the *Changes*, thus legitimating highly dubious documents.

As an example of how an Evidential Studies–oriented Qing scholar might gloss a passage related to an early *Changes* divination, consider Mao Qiling's (1623–1716) interpretation of an anecdote from the *Zuo Commentary* related in chapter 1—the defeat and arrest of Duke Hui of Jin by Duke Mu of Qin in 645 BCE. We can see in Mao's analysis the obvious legacy of Han-era techniques, which differ substantially from the original explanation offered by Duke Mu's diviner.

Mao begins by noting that the idea of "crossing a big river" in the judgment is derived from the lower four lines of Gu, which resemble the Kan trigram (the symbol of water) inasmuch as they consist of a pair of yang lines contained between two yin lines. In other words Mao interprets the four lowest lines visually as if they were three. Second, he points out that the upper nuclear trigram of Gu—that is, lines 3, 4, and 5—is Zhen, which is the symbol not only of a feudal lord but also of an upturned bowl resembling the body of a chariot. Since the upper primary trigram (Gen) is Zhen turned upside down, this indicates the overthrow of Duke Hui. And because Gen symbolizes both the hands and the idea of stoppage (according to the Explaining the Trigrams commentary), the meaning conveyed is clearly the arrest of Duke Hui. This notion is reinforced by consideration of the hexagram Sui (number 17), the opposite of Gu, in which the line readings refer repeatedly to tying someone up, presumably Duke Hui.[56]

Gu

Let us now jump briefly to the twentieth century before turning our attention in the next section to divination in late imperial times. In 1905, as part of a reform movement designed to modernize China in the aftermath of the disastrous Sino-Japanese War of 1894–95, the Qing government abolished the civil service examination system, which had reinforced Cheng-Zhu orthodoxy and the authority of the *Yijing* and other Confucian classics for nearly seven hundred years. Less than a decade later, the Qing dynasty itself fell to republican revolution, ending any semblance of official patronage of classical scholarship.

In this new postimperial environment, as in earlier periods, studies of the *Changes* followed the general contours of Chinese political, social, and intellectual life. For a time several classically trained Chinese scholars continued to analyze the *Yijing* in order to display their erudition, and a few "tradition-minded" individuals still viewed the document as a sacred scripture. At least one scholar, Wang Xiangxuan (fl. 1915), even wrote a syncretic book in Chinese titled *Unity of the Changes*, in which he attempted to reconcile Confucianism, Daoism, Buddhism, Islam, Judaism, and Christianity.[57] But Chinese intellectuals increasingly came to view the *Yijing* as simply a historical artifact—one that had no practical or spiritual value for contemporary Chinese society. Contributing mightily to this self-consciously secular approach to the *Changes* was a burst of Chinese scholarship based on new archaeological discoveries and a new-found fascination with the scientific method.[58]

Guo Moruo's (1892–1978) studies of the *Yijing*, beginning with his celebrated 1927 article "Life and Society in the Era of the *Zhou Changes*," marked the beginning of a long period in China during which Marxist categories and concerns played a major role in the analysis of the *Yijing*. Soon thereafter humanistic opponents of Marxist materialism, including Xiong Shili (1885–1968) and Fang Dongmei (1899–1977), began to champion the *Changes* as a means of revitalizing traditional Chinese thought, Confucianism in particular.

Following the establishment of the People's Republic of China in 1949 and until 1978, this intellectual struggle persisted as part of the larger political rivalry between the Chinese mainland and Taiwan. But intellectual liberalization in the PRC after 1978 vastly expanded the interpretive parameters of *Yijing* scholarship, as well as the scope of more popular writing. Confucianism (and, to a lesser degree, Buddhism and Daoism) was no longer a dirty word on the mainland, and the past increasingly seemed at least possibly relevant to the Chinese present and future. As a result, from the 1980s to today there has been a surge of interest in the *Changes* on both sides of the Taiwan Strait unprecedented since the Qing dynasty. And a significant part of this interest revolves around divination.

The *Changes* as a Divinatory Instrument: Some Case Studies from Late Imperial China

Throughout the entire imperial era and up to the present day, divinations involving the *Yijing* have sought to answer three basic questions: (1) What is the nature of the situation represented by the name, judgment, trigrams, and individual lines of the selected hexagram(s)? (2) What is one's position in this cosmically ordained situation in terms of time, place, and status? And (3) how can one determine one's best options and the best time(s) to act (or not act)?[59] Under some circumstances a hexagram may be chosen arbitrarily because it seems to suit a certain particular situation; indeed, there are books in Chinese that organize the sixty-four hexagrams according to themes such as self-cultivation, civil administration, military affairs, legal decisions, education, family matters, and dangerous situations. But technically speaking a true divination requires the construction of a hexagram line by line using milfoil stalks.[60]

The major model for orthodox milfoil divination in late imperial times, and especially the Qing period, was Zhu Xi's famous essay "Milfoil Etiquette," first published at the end of his *Fundamental Meaning of the Zhou Changes* and subsequently appended to a great many other works on the *Yijing*. Zhu's elaborate instructions, inspired in part by the Great Commentary, underscore the overtly spiritual dimension of *Yijing* consultation. He begins with a list of the necessary items for the ritual: a table of certain specified dimensions (located ideally in a secluded room), a divining board, an incense burner, incense, a container of fifty milfoil stalks, and writing materials (see figure 3.8).

According to Zhu, after engaging in preliminary ceremonies of ablution and purification, the diviner should enter the room from the east, approach the divining board (situated on a table oriented west to east), and burn incense to "show reverence." Then, taking the bundle of milfoil stalks from a container located to the north of the divining board, the person consulting the *Changes* holds the stalks with both hands and passes them through the smoke rising from the incense burner, located to the south of the container, below the board. The diviner then addresses the stalks: "Availing of you, great milfoil with constancy [i.e., reliability], I, official so-and-so, because of thus-and-such affair, wonder if I may express my doubts and concerns to the spiritual powers. Whether the news is auspicious or in-

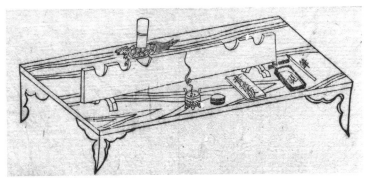

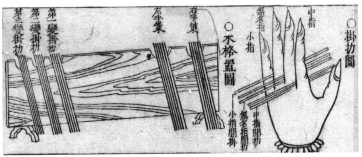

FIGURE 3.8

Illustrations of a Divination Table and
the Process of Milfoil Separation

Above, a rare excerpt from an eighteenth-century Japanese book
on the *Changes*, which shows a writing brush, an inkstone, an ink
stick, an incense burner, a wooden device for holding the
separated milfoil stalks, and a tubelike storage container for the
stalks. *Below*, another illustration from the same work depicts the
process of separating the stalks in the course of a divination. From
the Ni Tsieh Collection on *I Ching* Studies, University
of California, Irvine. Reproduced with permission from Special
Collections and Archives, Langson Library, University of
California, Irvine.

auspicious, involves a gain or a loss, remorse or humili-
ation, sorrow or anxiety, you alone with your divine
intelligence can provide clear information [about the
situation]."

Following this prayerlike statement, the diviner begins the elaborate process of dividing the stalks.[61] This
process eventually yields six lines, each of which is either yin (numbered six or eight) or yang (numbered
seven or nine). Lines numbered six or nine are considered to be changing into their opposites; thus they
yield a second hexagram to be taken into account.[62]
Although the evidence is fragmentary and largely an-
ecdotal, many literati diviners seem to have quite faith-
fully followed Zhu Xi's basic guidelines.

This may also have been true of Zhu's instructions
for examining the result, which appear in chapter 4 of
his *Introduction to the Study of the Changes*. He writes:
"Any hexagram may have all unchanging lines. In that
case we prognosticate on the basis of the original hexagram's judgment, taking the inner trigram as the question, or present situation, and the outer trigram as the
prognostication." When only one line changes, "we
take the statement of the original hexagram's changing
line as the prognostication." When two lines change,
"we take the statements of the two changing lines of
the original hexagram as the prognostication, but we
take the uppermost line as ruler." When three lines
change, "the prognostication involves the judgment of
the original hexagram and that of the resulting hexagram, using the original hexagram as the question or

general situation and the resulting hexagram as the prognostication." When four lines change, "we use the two unchanging lines in the resulting hexagram as the prognostication, but we take the lower line as the ruler." When five lines change, "we use the unchanging line of the resulting hexagram as the prognostication." When all six lines change, if the hexagrams are Qian (number 1) and Kun (number 2), the prognostications of both are used. For other hexagrams, "the prognostication is the judgment of the resulting hexagram."[63]

The evidence strongly suggests, however, that there was no general agreement on how to interpret the results of an *Yijing* divination. For instance some commentators maintain that if a hexagram has no changing lines, the diviner need take into account not only the judgment but also the Commentary on the Judgments and the overall Commentary on the Images. If any lines are changing, special attention should be given to the line statements and the Commentary on the Images pertaining to those lines, as well as to the judgment, the Commentary on the Judgments, and the overall Commentary on the Images of the derivative hexagram. Some *Yijing* specialists argue that regardless of how many lines of a hexagram have changed, the derivative hexagram should be taken into account, but others maintain that a hexagram cannot be considered "transformed" unless three or more of its lines are either "old yang" (nine) or "old yin" (six).

Furthermore, we know that some diviners emphasized judgments exclusively, while others placed primary emphasis on trigrams and trigram relationships, including nuclear trigrams. Still others focused primarily on lines and line statements, sometimes in highly idiosyncratic ways (for example the late Qing diviner Chen Maohou always emphasized the fifth line in any given hexagram). Some diviners paid special attention to laterally linked lines in both trigrams and hexagrams, and some naturally used a combination of techniques.

Regardless of what a diviner might choose to emphasize in any given instance, there remained a host of interpretive possibilities—at least as many as there were in the realm of textual criticism. To be sure, one's choices might be shaped by prevailing conventions, but all Chinese scholars understood, at least as a matter of principle, that in divination, as in textual interpretation, a thorough understanding of any given judgment, hexagram, trigram, or line required a command of all major commentaries. The most comprehensive extant collection of this sort remains Li Guangdi's imperially endorsed *Balanced Compendium on the Zhou Changes* (1715). Although this latter work emphasizes the state's Cheng-Zhu orthodoxy, it also provides a broad range of scholarly opinions on the *Yijing*—eighteen from the Han dynasty, five from the Six Dynasties period, one from the Sui, eleven from the Tang, ninety-eight from the Song, two from the Jin, twenty-two from the Yuan, and sixty-one from the Ming.

The Kangxi emperor (r. 1662–1722), who commissioned the *Balanced Compendium on the Zhou Changes*, was especially devoted to the classic. As he once remarked: "I have never tired of the *Yijing*, and have used it in fortune-telling and as a source of moral principles."[64] The official "Account of Imperial Activities" and the "Veritable Records" for the Kangxi emperor's reign provide many concrete illustrations of his use of the *Changes*, both for specific advice and for general guidance. Let us examine a few such cases.

By 1680, at the age of twenty-six, the Kangxi emperor had begun a careful reading of the *Yijing* together with his court lecturers, spending three days on each hexagram. The official account of the emperor's activities for December 12 of that year reveals one of the ways in which the *Changes* figured in Kangxi's daily schedule of work and study. As usual the emperor began his day with a dawn meeting to discuss matters of state with his grand secretaries and other high officials. Later in the morning the emperor received his court lecturers—Kulena, Ye Fan'gai, and Zhang Yushu in this case—at the Mouqin Hall to study and discuss the primary trigram images of Zhen (thunder) and Li (fire) in the hexagram Shihe ("Bite Together," number 21). They considered in particular the cryptic first line statement, which reads: "Made to wear whole foot shackles, his toes are destroyed, but he will be without blame."[65]

After the lecture Kulena made a special point of emphasizing how the meaning of each line statement was contingent on its position in any given hexagram but that it was important to understand the meaning of the hexagram as a whole before examining the meaning of its constituent elements. He also presented the emperor with a text discussing the symbolic significance of the hexagrams Qian (number 1) and Kun (number 2). After examining this document, the emperor redirected his attention to the Shihe hexagram, which usually refers to criminal cases, observing that the fourth line represented the person meting out punishment, while the top and bottom lines in this case represented those receiving punishment. He seems to have had in mind two pressing judicial matters that had been discussed earlier in the morning and was presumably encouraged by the fourth line of Shihe, which indicates that "It is fitting that one have good fortune here in exercising perseverance in the face of difficulties."[66]

The Kangxi emperor often consulted the *Changes* on matters relating to punishment. For instance, in 1683, after Taiwan had just been recaptured from rebel forces under the descendents of Zheng Chenggong (1624–62), the emperor and his court lecturers discussed the image of the Lü hexagram ("The Wanderer," number 56), in which the Li trigram, signifying fire, rests on top of the Gen trigram, representing a mountain. The Commentary on the Images reads: "Above the Mountain there is fire; this constitutes the image of the Wanderer [Lü]. In the same way, the superior man uses punishments with enlightenment and care, and does not protract cases at law."[67] To Kangxi, the calm of the mountain signified the need for care, while fire, which spreads rapidly, indicated that legal matters should be settled quickly and decisively.

During 1684, in the course of studying the *Yijing* with his court lecturers, the Kangxi emperor noticed that they had placed in the category of "things there was no need to discuss" the sixth line of the Qian hexagram (number 1), which reads: "A dragon that [arrogantly] overreaches should have cause for regret." The emperor pointed out, however, that the Commentary on the Words of the Text for the top line of Qian reads: "The expression 'overreaches' means that one knows how to advance but not how to retreat, knows how to preserve life but not to relinquish it, knows how to gain but not to lose. How could such a one ever be a sage?"[68] He went on to tell his court lecturers that "everything follows this principle as it is expressed in the *Changes*, that arrogance will lead to sorrow. We should by rights take this as a warning; it is not something we should shy away from."

The Kangxi emperor's interpretation of the hexagram Feng ("Abundance," number 55) provides yet another illustration of the way in which the Son of Heaven probed more deeply into the *Yijing* than his formalized lectures and discussions required. The basic judgment of Feng appears highly favorable: "Abundance means prevalence, which the true king extends to the utmost. Stay free from worry, and you shall be fit to be a sun at midday."[69] Yet in contemplating the hexagram, the Kangxi emperor emphasized that the circumstances defined by Feng in fact ebb and flow. He cited the Commentary on the Judgments, which states: "When the sun is at midday, it begins to set, and when the moon is at its full, it begins to wane. As everything in Heaven and Earth waxes and wanes at the proper moment, is this not even truer for men, even truer for gods and spirits?"[70] He also paid particular attention to the line statement of the yang line in the third position: "The underbrush is of such abundance that the small stars can be seen at noon."[71] This statement, he remarked, warns of petty people who push themselves forward and prevent more able men from undertaking significant work. Kangxi's response was to give special consideration to personnel matters under the circumstances.

In 1688, during a severe spring drought and in the midst of factional struggle at court, the Kangxi emperor ordered his diviners to consult the *Yijing*. They selected the hexagram Kuai ("Resolution," number 43), which refers to a "breakthrough," as in nature when a cloudburst occurs, or in human affairs when inferior people begin to disperse. The line statements of greatest concern to the emperor were those connected to the yang lines in the third and fifth places. The former line statement reads in part: "The exemplary person acts with perfect Resolution. But if he should encounter such a rain that it would be as if he were sunk in water, and though he [might] feel anger [because of criticism], there will be no one to blame." The latter line statement reads: "The pokeweed is dispatched with perfect resolution. If this one treads the middle path, he shall be without blame."[72] From these indications the emperor determined that a purge of the bureaucracy was necessary, and he therefore removed from office all the senior members of Grand Secretary Mingju's threatening clique.

Like the emperor, Chinese officials regularly resorted to *Yijing* divination, undertaken either by themselves or by others (both professionals and amateurs).[73] Often the incentive was military exigency. During the 1780s, for instance, the Manchu commander Fukang'an (d. 1796) faced a difficult military decision in the war against Muslim rebels and ordered Luo Shijing, a high degree holder with considerable divinatory skill, to employ the *Changes*. Luo selected the hexagram Jin ("Advance," number 35), which, because it refers to the "Marquis of Kang"—the same *kang* ("peace and prosperity") that appears in Fukang'an's name—and because the hexagram as a whole denotes progress and success, was viewed as a highly favorable omen, encouraging the general to persevere. It proved to be, and when the revolt was finally suppressed, Fukang'an received the rank of marquis from the throne.[74]

Sun Yiyan was a high degree holder who became prefect of Anqing in 1858. At that time the city was threatened by the Taiping rebels, and Sun received timely inspiration and guidance from his study of the *Yijing*, particularly the hexagram Mingyi ("Suppression of the Light," number 36). This hexagram usually refers to a situation in which threatening circumstances require caution and inner strength, despite great difficulties and the criticism of others. Eventually the darkness yields to light and goodness triumphs.[75]

As indicated by Sun's divination, the Taipings were repulsed from Anqing and before too long the movement collapsed. This sequence of events confirmed his widely, if not universally, shared belief that the *Yijing* "makes foreknowledge possible."

Of course the *Changes* could also serve nonmilitary purposes. During the late eighteenth century, for example, Ma Jinzhi, an *Yijing* specialist from a town near Shanghai, was asked by his fellow townspeople to divine about the prospects for building a new bridge in a place where local conditions and problems with funding made construction difficult. He divined and got the Guimei ("Marrying Maid," number 54) hexagram, with an emphasis on the second line: "As a one-eyed person who can keep on seeing, how fitting is the perseverance of this secluded one." Although Guimei is usually associated with husband-wife relationships, Ma applied it to the local project. He drew particular inspiration from the first line: "If this one as a lame person can still keep on treading, to set forth here would mean good fortune."[76] With this encouragement, which seems to have resulted in timely financial aid, local leaders found their way clear to build the bridge.

As a means of "resolving doubts," the *Yijing*, like other forms of Chinese divination, could promote action or counsel patience, inspire dedication or encourage passive resignation. In the late Ming period, for example, Lü Gong (1603–64) divined regarding his future at a potential turning point in his scholarly ca-

reer. He selected the hexagram Pi (number 12) changing to Tai (number 11). Pi signifies decline—a time in
which "the great depart, and the petty arrive"—a period of retreat and seclusion. Tai, on the other hand,
indicates a point at which "the petty depart and the
great arrive." Lü therefore bided his time, engaging in
study, travel, and contemplation. After the Ming dynasty fell and the Qing was established, Lü divined
again. This time he selected Qian (number 1), with an
emphasis on the yang line in the second place: "When
a dragon appears in the fields, it is fitting to see the
great man."[77] Prodded into action by this highly auspicious omen, Lü participated in the grand imperial examination of 1647 and took highest honors. He subsequently embarked on a distinguished career as a Qing
official and became a grand secretary in 1654.

Accounts by Western observers in nineteenth-century China indicate that *Yijing*-inspired methods of
divination continued to be ubiquitous at all levels of
society. The well-informed missionary John Nevius,
for instance, recounts a ritual that suggests certain aspects of Zhu Xi's orthodox model, although the diviner employs the disparaged "coin system" to derive a
hexagram rather than the far more time-consuming
process of separating milfoil stalks. Nevius writes:

> When a person wishing a response presents himself
> [to the fortune-teller], a small box, containing
> three copper cash, is handed to him, which he takes
> very reverently in both hands, and with which he

describes a circle around incense-sticks burning before paintings of the patrons of the art of divination. After having made his prostrations before
these paintings, he proceeds in the same reverent
manner to the door, and then invokes the aid of
heaven, in a form somewhat like the following: "To
day, I _____, residing near the temple _____, on
account of sickness in my family (or some other
cause, as the case may be), present myself to obtain
a true response respecting this matter. Let me
know the event, whether it be favorable, or the
contrary." This ceremony being performed, the applicant places the box with cash in the hands of the
diviner, who also, after asking a few questions,
waves it with even greater solemnity over the table
of incense. He then repeats a form of prayer, generally addressed to the patrons of the mystic art. The
form prescribed . . . is the following: "Though
Heaven has no voice, when addressed, there is a response; the gods are living, and when invoked, are
near. A man is now present who is harassed with
anxieties, and is unable to solve his doubts and per-
plexities. We can only look to the gods to instruct
us as to what is or is not to take place."[78]

For guidance in forming his interpretation, Nevius
reports that the fortune-teller consulted a book that
appears to be Wang Weide's well-known and widely
used diviner's manual titled *Orthodox Divination*, first
published in 1709. According to Nevius, after the con-

sulting process was completed, the fortune-teller wrote down the hexagram along with its explanation and handed it to the inquirer, who might then have it interpreted a second time by another diviner. Payment, he says, differed according to "the circumstances of the applicant and the importance of the matter in hand."[79]

The Transnational Travels of the *Yijing*

Everyone knows how rapidly religious ideas and works of art and literature circulate in the modern world. We sometimes forget, however, that the globalization of culture has been occurring for centuries, and without it there would obviously be no "world religions" or even the concept of "world literature." How, we might ask, do texts and ideas travel across boundaries of space and time, and what happens to them in the process? Clearly, for an idea or a text to move from one culture area to another, and to have staying power, it must have some sort of intellectual, aesthetic, emotional, or spiritual appeal. By definition great religious traditions such as Islam, Judaism, Christianity, Hinduism, and Buddhism—and their foundational texts—meet this standard. But the circumstances under which they travel, and the conditions under which they take hold, vary enormously from time to time and culture to culture.[1]

Texts and ideas constantly evolve, and as they move across borders the process accelerates, often dramatically. Nowhere is this process more obvious than when texts are translated. Proverbially, all "translators are traitors," but there are different forms of literary treason, and different motives that lie behind them. In the hands of some translators, a text can become nothing more than a device for promoting a certain political, social, intellectual, or religious point of view, a form of "cultural imperialism."[2] But a skilled translator can offer a version of the text that captures both the allure of its ideas and the beauty of its language without significant distortion, thus opening new avenues of cross-cultural understanding.[3] Goethe once claimed, for example, that a French translation of his masterpiece, *Faust*, made the work "again fresh, new and spirited."[4]

With these basic ideas and issues in mind, let us look now at the transnational travels of the *Yijing*, paying special attention to how and why it moved, and how it became domesticated in various environments, both Asian and Western. We will also look briefly at some of the many and sometimes surprising ways that the *Changes* has influenced world culture, past and present.

The *Changes* in East Asia

Although the specific circumstances under which the *Yijing* found its way to various East Asian countries naturally differed, there seem to be certain similarities in the way that it traveled. In the first place, from the early centuries of the common era into the late nineteenth century, the classical Chinese written language was the lingua franca of virtually all literate elites in Korea, Japan, and Vietnam, employed in a fashion roughly analogous to the scholarly use of Latin in the West; thus there was no need to translate it—except, on occasion, to render it in a more vernacular form to make it somewhat more accessible to commoners. Second, during this same period, intellectual life in all three areas came to be shaped in significant ways by the broad, albeit constantly evolving, patterns of Confucian, Daoist, and Buddhist thought in China. Third, since the *Yijing* continued to occupy an exalted position in China for some two thousand years, into the twentieth century, there was never a time when it lacked prestige in these peripheral areas. A fourth feature of the process by which various East Asian peoples borrowed from Chinese culture was their periodic use of emissaries—individuals and groups who visited China and brought back Chinese texts and traditions to their home countries in a self-conscious and sometimes quite systematic way. But once such texts arrived, their interaction with indigenous ideas and institutions produced significant variations.

The Interplay between Local and Borrowed Cultural Forms

From about 1400 CE to the late nineteenth century, the dominant cultural agents of China (literati and wealthy merchants), Japan (hereditary samurai and wealthy merchants), Korea (hereditary *yangban* aristocrats), and Vietnam (rural literati) all enthusiastically embraced the fundamental values associated with various strands of Confucianism.[1] Although this particular brand of learning might have been initially identified with Chinese culture, it transcended space and ethnicity. Alien conquerors of China, such as the Mongols and Manchus, employed it selectively for their own purposes, as did the Japanese, Koreans, and Vietnamese.[2]

The elites who ruled Choson (or Joseon) Korea (1392–1910), as well as those who held sway over Le (1428–1789) and early Nguyen (1802–1945) dynasty Vietnam, were substantially different in many ways from their counterparts in China—even though the governments of both states chose their officials (and also reinforced their orthodoxies) by means of civil service examinations written in classical Chinese. In Tokugawa Japan (1600–1868), where there was no such examination system, the intellectual independence of the samurai class was especially great. Thus, although the Tokugawa shoguns eventually selected Zhu Xi's Neo-Confucianism as their official orthodoxy, there was no significant institutional reinforcement of it.[3]

In Choson Korea, the examination system, modeled generally after the Ming-Qing system, was theoretically open to commoners, but in fact it was generally limited to yangban, who, by some accounts, had to demonstrate repeatedly their allegiance to Cheng-Zhu orthodoxy in both word and deed. At the same time, however, the Choson examinations often prized literary (especially poetic) skills to a greater degree than did their Chinese counterparts, and occasionally the examination questions departed from the state orthodoxy.[4]

The Vietnamese examination system followed the Chinese model in certain respects, but the Vietnamese system was not truly countrywide, and printed books were in chronically short supply. At times the Vietnamese exams were somewhat more practical than those of the Chinese or Koreans, and on occasion they included Daoist and Buddhist as well as Confucian content. Moreover, Vietnam lacked China's and Korea's "academy-based scholastic warfare." Village organizations provided the basic environment for Confucian learning in Vietnam, with the result that they were much more likely than academies to tolerate un-orthodox popular ideas and eclectic formulations.[5]

In each East Asian setting, then, institutionalized Confucianism took different forms, interacting with other belief systems, including Buddhism, Daoism, and indigenous religions, in complex ways. The situation in Tibet was complicated for somewhat different reasons. Varying degrees of Chinese overlordship in this diverse and isolated area during the Yuan, Ming, and Qing dynasties did virtually nothing to Confu-cianize Tibetan culture, which remained steadfastly Buddhist in character, dominated by clerics known as *lamas* (lit., "superior ones"). There was, however, a considerable degree of interaction between Chinese and Tibetan elites at various times, which resulted in a two-way flow of cultural influences. Several Chinese emperors took an interest in Tibetan Buddhism, par-ticularly during the Qing period, and at least some Ti-betan lamas gravitated toward certain Chinese philo-sophical texts, including the *Changes*.

With this brief overview as background, let us now look at the various ways that the *Yijing* came to be transmitted and transformed in Japan, Korea, Viet-nam, and Tibet during the past several hundred years.

Japan

The Japanese case is comparatively well-known.[6] The *Changes* found its way to Japan no later than the sixth century CE, but it was not until the seventeenth century that interest in the document blossomed. From the beginning of the Tokugawa Shogunate in 1600 to the fall of the regime in 1868, more than a thousand books were written on the *Changes*—an amount not much less than the total number of books written on the *Yijing* during the more or less contemporary Qing period in China—a country with a population about fifteen times greater than Japan's.

In part the outburst of Japanese writing on the *Changes* had to do with roughly contemporary scholarly fashions in China. But it also had a practical political dimension. From the very beginning of the Tokugawa era, the *Yijing* was used to bolster and amplify Tokugawa Confucianism. In the early Tokugawa period, many emperors and shoguns sought spiritual and practical guidance in the *Changes*. For instance Shogun Tsunayoshi, who ruled from 1680 to 1709, presided over at least 240 *Yijing* seminars in one seven-year period. In these seminars, Tsunayoshi sometimes gave his own lectures on Zhu Xi's *Fundamental Meaning of the Zhou Changes* to audiences consisting of not only his close retainers but also daimyo and other high-ranking samurai, local administrative personnel, executive officials, Buddhist monks, and Shinto priests.[7]

The *Yijing* was often used to support the central Confucian notion of loyalty to the ruler. Thus we find Matsunaga Sekigo writing in the seventeenth century: "The *Classic of Changes* reads: 'At the beginning, we had Heaven and Earth, then husband and wife followed. Father and son came after husband and wife. Ruler and subject came after father and son.' Who can live without these relationships? If you apply filial piety to your parents to serve your ruler, it becomes loyalty. Using the method of settling family affairs to govern the country will bring peace and stability."[8]

The *Changes* could also explain the shogun's unique position as a ruler administering the realm in the emperor's name. Another seventeenth-century Japanese writer, Asayama Soshin, tells us: "Of the six unbroken lines [of the Qian hexagram, number 1], the lord's place is indicated by the second line from the top, the fifth from the bottom. Why not the first line at the very top, as some would argue? If the ruler of the realm thinks that he is the top of everything . . . he should be told that this is clearly contrary to the Way of Heaven, that he will do evil things. The place at the top has the following negative commentary in the *Yijing*: 'A dragon at the top will have cause to repent.'"[9] Actually the top line statement says only that the dragon who "overreaches" (i.e., is "arrogant") will have cause for regret, but the point remained that it was all right for the emperor to be at the top because he did not rule, he merely reigned.

The *Yijing* could be used to validate or undergird other Japanese cultural traditions as well—including both native Shinto and borrowed Buddhism. Buddhists, for instance, often explained the idea of reincarnation in terms of the following passage from the

CHAPTER 4

Great Commentary of the *Changes*: "We trace things back to their origins then turn back to their ends. Thus we understand the axiom of life and death. With the consolidation of material force [qi] into essence, a person comes into being, but with the dissipation of one's spirit, change comes about. It is due to this that we understand the true state of gods and spirits."[10] Similarly, Shinto scholars sought to validate their belief system by reference to the *Changes*. A common strategy was to cite the Commentary on the Judgments for the Guan hexagram ("Viewing," number 20), which reads: "Viewing the Way of the Spirits [pronounced *Shendao* in Chinese and *Shinto* in Japanese], one finds that the four seasons never deviate, and so the sage establishes his teachings on the basis of ... [this Way], and all under Heaven submit to him."[11]

There were, of course, other ways of linking the *Yijing* to indigenous Shinto beliefs. Kumazawa Banzan (1619–91) wrote:

> The Way of the sages in China is also the Way of the Spirits. Shinto in my country [Japan] is the Shinto of Heaven and Earth. The *Changes* is also the Shinto of Heaven and Earth.... The Chinese sage known as Fuxi was the first to draw the lines of the Qian trigram and the Kun trigram, which later developed into the eight trigrams and eventually became the sixty-four hexagrams. Similarly, we [Japanese] have used the number eight, such as the Yata no [Mirror] and the Yasaka [Jade], because

the Shinto of Heaven and Earth is one, and it is naturally the same wonderful principle shared by both Japan and China.[12]

As in other areas of East Asia during the same period, Zhu Xi's interpretations of the *Yijing* were considered orthodox during much of the Tokugawa period, but this did not prevent scholars in Japan, Korea, or Vietnam from criticizing Cheng-Zhu orthodoxy, using the Evidential Studies approach of contemporary Chinese critics as well as their own distinctive methodologies.[13] An excellent example is the wide-ranging scholarship of Ito Togai (1670–1736), whose *Comprehensive Explanation of the Text and the Ten Wings of the Zhou Changes*—part of a long family tradition of *Yijing*-related research—has been described as the most important single work written on the classic in Japan during the entire Tokugawa period. In this book and others, Ito systematically dismantled several commonly accepted opinions about the *Yijing*, including the idea that Confucius was the author of the Ten Wings.[14]

Not surprisingly the *Yijing* inspired Japanese imitations, as it had done in China and would do also in Korea. One such work was Yamaga Soko's (1622–85) numerologically oriented *Exploring the Origins of Things and Our Impulses to Action*, a work reminiscent of Shao Yong's *Supreme Principles That Rule the World* and explicitly designed to convey the essence of the *Changes*. Rather than drawing on the eight trigrams, however, Yamaga employed eight esoteric symbols that resemble fragments of Japan's indigenously developed Kana syllabary—symbols that he used to "convey the essential forms of change in history."[15] Yamaga is well-known for his view that Japan rather than China was the center and apex of civilization, and that the two Japanese deities, Izanagi and Izanami, were in fact the foundations of the concepts of yin and yang.

As these few examples suggest, individuals of all outlooks and backgrounds embraced the *Yijing* in Tokugawa Japan—not only Confucians, Buddhists, and Shinto clergy, but also exponents of "Ancient Learning," so-called Mito scholars (emphasizing reverence for the emperor), and advocates of Western ideas or "Dutch Learning." As a result the *Changes* penetrated all levels of Japanese society. Samurai scholars and members of the clergy studied the *Changes* and also divined with it; merchants used the *Yijing* to make all kinds of business decisions (there were even commercial divination manuals that used the sixty-four hexagrams of the *Yijing* to predict price fluctuations in the rice market), and as a justification for their profession. Manuals prepared for artisans explained crafts such as shipbuilding and architecture in terms of the *Changes*, and peasants throughout the land conducted their daily lives in accordance with the dictates of professional fortune-tellers and *Yijing*-influenced almanacs.[16]

In Japanese high culture, as in Chinese society, the symbolism of the *Changes* appeared everywhere—from artistic, literary, and musical criticism to popular drama, the tea ceremony, flower arranging, and board games. Its symbolism also played a significant role in Japanese science, technology, medicine, and military affairs—again, as it did in these same realms of Chinese culture. Even distinctly Japanese cultural forms, such as *tanka* poetry (consisting of five lines of thirty-one syllables, broken down 5-7-5-7-7), came to be explained in terms of *Yijing* numerical categories.

Over time the *Yijing* became increasingly assimilated to the indigenous culture of Japan, at least in some circles. Thus we find Jiun Sonja (1718–1804), a nativist scholar, arguing that the images of the Yellow River Chart (which by some accounts provided the model for the eight trigrams) were manifested through the Okitsu Mirror, a round bronze object kept at the sacred Ise shrine. According to Jiun, the authors of the *Changes* "copied our ancient divination of Takam-ga-hara [a place in the "high heaven" where Izanagi and Izanami lived] in formulating its text and style. The whole book is completely borrowed from us [the Japa-

FIGURE 4.1
An *Yijing*-Inspired Japanese Painting: Uragami Gyokudo's (1745–1820) *Reading the* Changes *Sitting by a Mountain Waterfall* This large painting (ca. 168.1 × 92.4 cm) displays a number of characteristic features of Chinese-style landscapes—steep mountains, flowing water, and abundant foliage. It also contains some quite unusual features, notably the several circular, plateaulike outcroppings. The person consulting the *Changes* occupies a tiny hut near the bottom of the painting, midway between the two sides. Reproduced with permission from the Okayama Prefectural Museum of Art.

nese]."[17] Hirata Atsutane (1776–1843), for his part, went so far as to assert that the ancient Chinese culture hero Fuxi, putative inventor of the trigrams, was actually a Shinto deity.[18]

Although the *Yijing* was often cited to support the political status quo, it could also be used to justify political reform. Thus we have Ito Jinsai (1627–1705) using the Ge hexagram ("Radical Change," number 49) to explain the need for new solutions to contemporary problems: "If the sages of the past lived in today's world," he wrote, "they would have to act according to today's customs, and apply today's laws. Therefore, [the *Classic of Changes* says,] 'When the great man does a leopard change, it means that his pattern [i.e., culture] becomes magnificent, and when the petty man radically changes his countenance, it means he will follow his sovereign with obedience.' Thus, the country will naturally be well governed."[19]

Eventually, as the Tokugawa rulers began to lose their political authority in the mid-nineteenth century, the *Yijing* was increasingly used to attack the shogunate. Hirose Tanso (1782–1856), focusing on hexagram number 12 [Pi in Chinese, "Obstruction"] wrote, for example, that the arrangement of the trigrams in this hexagram (with Qian, "Heaven," at the top and Kun, "Earth," below) indicated a kind of cosmological blockage, signifying that the sovereign and his subjects were not in harmony. This, he said, symbolized a country "without proper rule." He went on to argue that the ruling warrior family (i.e., the shogunate) had made the mistake of arrogantly creating too much distance between above and below, making communication impossible.[20]

In 1868 the Tokugawa Shogunate fell, owing to the self-sacrifice of revolutionaries such as Yoshida Shoin (1830–59), whose use of the *Yijing* to express his personal and political opinions is well documented. In prison, awaiting execution for his revolutionary activities, Yoshida composed the following poignant verse:

> With nothing to do in prison,
> I contemplate the principles of the *Yijing*
> to understand the principles of change.
> Through the hole of this broken hut,
> I sometimes look up and watch the clouds floating by.[21]

Korea

In Korea, as in Japan, the influence of the *Changes* was pervasive. Because the governments in both of these neighboring states drew heavily upon various Confucian traditions of scholarship and rulership from the early sixteenth century into the late nineteenth, the *Yijing* occupied a prominent place in all elite discourses. As in Japan, it had wide application at every level of Korean society, extending into the realms of language, philosophy, religion, art, music, literature, science, medicine, and social customs. It also played a major role in the geomantic traditions of Korea, as it did in all other areas of East Asia.[22]

The *Yijing* found its way to Korea no later than the fourth century CE (some argue it arrived several centuries earlier), but it was not until the Choson period (1392–1910) that its influence began to spread dramatically. During most of this time, the Korean government solidly supported an orthodox Cheng-Zhu–style Neo-Confucianism based on the Chinese model. But over time, as in Japan and Vietnam, Korean scholars embraced all the philosophical options that developed in China from the Song dynasty through the Qing. Moreover, they developed distinctive interpretations of their own.[23]

The same was naturally true in the narrower but increasingly important realm of *Yijing* scholarship. Some scholars have viewed the writings of So Kyongdok (also known as Hwadam; 1489–1546), inspired in part by the cosmological speculations of the Song dynasty scholar Shao Yong and others, as the foundation of Korean "*Changes* Studies." Hwadam was an early exponent of the idea that qi, generated in the form of yin and yang by the Supreme Ultimate, actually created material objects, and that this creative process was only "guided" by principle.[24] In other words, he believed that the physical substance of things was more important than the cosmic "principle" that endowed these things with their distinctive natures. But Hwadam's materialist views met powerful resistance from more orthodox Neo-Confucian thinkers such as Yi Hwang

(1501–70), known more generally in both Korea and the West by his pen name, T'oegye[25] (see figure 4.2).

T'oegye, often considered to be the most influential philosopher in all of Korean history, vigorously defended most of Zhu Xi's Neo-Confucian ideas, including the notion that the principle of things had priority over the material force (qi) of which they were constituted.[26] His intellectual support for Zhu Xi is evident in several of T'oegye's many *Yijing*-related lectures and writings, which attempted to systematize Neo-Confucian learning in Korea and to clarify certain obscure passages in Zhu's *Introduction to the Study of the Changes*. T'oegye's works were reprinted at least twice in Japan, where they had a considerable influence on Tokugawa scholarship.[27]

Yi Yulgok (1536–84), one of T'oegye's students, tried to strike a middle position between that of his teacher and various qi-oriented Korean scholars such as So Kyongdok and Ki Taesung (1527–72). On the one hand, he acknowledged the theoretical primacy of principle over material force, but on the other, he argued for a complex, situation-based relationship between the two, with no beginning and no end. Although he accepted the distinction made in the Great Commentary of the *Yijing* between what was "above physical form" ("the Way") and what was "below physical form" ("concrete objects"), he saw principle not as prior to material force but rather as the reason for it.[28]

Similarly Yulgok believed that although Heaven and human beings shared the same "sincerity," they

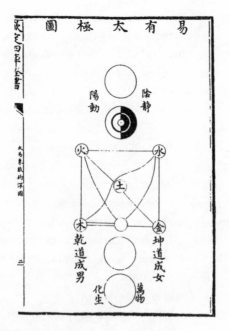

FIGURE 4.2

The Generative Power of the Supreme Ultimate
This Qing dynasty diagram, made famous by the Chinese
philosopher Zhou Dunyi (1017–73) and widely distributed
throughout Choson Korea (it appears prominently, for instance,
on the wall of T'oegye's reconstructed Pottery Mountain
Academy), shows how the Supreme Ultimate generates yin and
yang, which, in their ebb and flow and interaction, produce qi. Qi
becomes manifest in various combinations of the five agents
(depicted on the corners and in the middle of the square), and it
in turn becomes the stuff of which all things, animate and
inanimate, are constituted. The question that *Yijing* scholars
throughout East Asia constantly debated was the exact relationship between the "principle" of these things (a kind of Platonic
ideal) and the qi of which they were constituted.

were nonetheless distinguishable, as evidenced in the Qian hexagram (number 1). According to Yulgok the four characters that make up Qian's judgment—*yuan*, *heng, li,* and *zhen*—were the Heavenly counterparts to the "Four Beginnings" of human nature (benevolence, moral duty, ritual propriety, and humane knowledge) identified and celebrated by the great Chinese philosopher Mencius (372–289 BCE). To Yulgok the Qian hexagram must be interpreted as both the creative (moral) power of the cosmos and the creative action of the (moral) leader, who, by his sincerity, "awakens [people] and develops their higher nature."[29]

Another particularly interesting Korean thinker who sought to reconcile Neo-Confucian dichotomies was Chang Hyon-gwang (also known as Yohon, 1554–1637). Chang used the metaphor of weaving to illustrate the relationship between principle and material force. As he explained it, principle was the warp of unchanging substance, while material force was the woof of variable application. Both were part of a single Way. Similarly nature and emotion were interrelated rather than separate. Chang also believed—in the fashion of the Chinese philosopher Cheng Hao (1032–85)—that the principle of Heaven and Earth and all things was contained in the mind, making knowledge of everything possible.[30] For much of his adult life, Chang dedicated himself wholeheartedly to studying the *Yijing*. According to popular legend, he neither ate nor slept while so engaged. He wrote at least three influential books on the *Changes*, one of which was based on a series of lectures he gave to the Korean emperor on the political ethics of the *Yijing*.[31]

The point to be emphasized once again is that much of the scholarship on the *Changes*, whether Chinese, Japanese, Korean, or Vietnamese, defies the usual simplistic categories. Although Chang's writings are suffused with themes identified with the Chinese school of *Yijing* interpretation known as Meanings and Principles, they also reflect an abiding interest in the approach known as the School of Images and Numbers. And although Chang thoroughly embraced the methodological concerns of the School of Evidential Studies, he also emphasized statecraft and practical affairs.[32]

All of Chang's works on the *Changes* display enormous erudition. He was an extremely broad-ranging scholar who thoroughly investigated virtually every issue that had arisen in Chinese *Yijing* studies up to his own time. Although he accepted many orthodox ideas of the Cheng-Zhu school, he also disagreed with Zhu Xi and others on specific points, arguing, for example, that the theory of doubling that produced the sixty-four hexagrams from yin and yang was inconsistent. He also engaged in extremely detailed textual criticism, pointing out mistakes in previous Chinese and Korean scholarship and suggesting alternative readings.[33]

Chang's *Illustrated Explanation of Changes Scholarship* provides an excellent example of the enthusiasm Choson scholars had for *Yijing*-related diagrams. It also reveals Chang's own fascination with the Yellow River

Chart and the Luo River Writing, derivative illustrations of which occupy one entire chapter of this nine-chapter work. Many of the diagrams in his book are organized according to particular philosophical themes, such as the Supreme Ultimate, Heaven and Earth, the Sun and the Moon, Yin and Yang, the Five Agents, Creation, Categories of Things, and the Decrees of Heaven. Chang also includes individual essays on topics such as the deployment of troops, in which he draws on the judgment and the first line statement of the Shi hexagram ("Army," number 7) to argue for the importance of order and discipline in military affairs.

Later in his book Chang devotes attention to the alleged precursors of the *Changes*, such as the *Linked Mountains* and *Return to the Hidden*, as well as works inspired by the *Yijing*, such as Yang Xiong's *Classic of Great Mystery*. His illustrated analysis of the *Mystery* is particularly detailed and insightful, involving critical comparisons not only with the *Changes* itself but also with the numerologically oriented work of Chinese scholars such as Jing Fang and Shao Yong.

During the eighteenth and nineteenth centuries, "Solid Learning" (also called Han Learning or Evidential Studies) became popular in Korea, as it had been somewhat earlier in China. Downplaying metaphysics in favor of textual criticism, scholars of Solid Learning used the images and numbers of the *Changes* in creative new ways. Kim Sokmun (1658–1735), for example, tried to employ the *Yijing* to explain newly introduced Western scientific concepts, including the rotation of the earth and Ptolemaic astronomy. Significantly, he argued (in the fashion of Chinese scholars such as Fang Yizhi and Jiang Yong) that all natural phenomena can be represented by the symbolism of the *Yijing*.[34]

Chong Yagyong (Tasan, 1762–1836) was another powerful advocate of Western science and Solid Learning in Choson Korea. He wrote three highly regarded books on the *Changes*, all of which employed rigorous philological methods and broke new interpretive ground. Chong was a particularly exacting and scientifically minded scholar, whose meticulous scholarship brought Korean philological approaches to the classic to new heights.[35] But unlike most Evidential Studies scholars in China, he admired Zhu Xi's *Basic Meaning of the Zhou Changes* and was harshly critical of a good deal of Han dynasty scholarship—especially the writings of Zheng Xuan.[36] Chong was also critical of a great many other famous Chinese scholars: Wang Bi and Han Kangbo for their Daoist leanings; Tang literati for being either trivial, dry, or careless; Shao Yong for being too esoteric; Cheng Yi for relying too heavily on Wang Bi; Lai Zhide for making too many mistakes; Li Guangdi for betraying Zhu Xi's teachings in his capacity as the editor of the *Balanced Compendium on the Zhou Changes*; and Mao Qiling for "collecting the leftover words of the ancients to block the great achievements of Master Zhu [Xi]."[37]

Chong's critique of so much of Chinese scholarship on the *Changes* reflects an attitude prevalent among late Choson Confucians that "legitimate Confucianism could no longer be found in China but was preserved in Korea."[38] This sort of cultural pride was also expressed in what has been described as "Jizi worship."[39] Since Jizi ("Viscount Ji")—an upright uncle of the evil last ruler of the Shang dynasty, Zhou Xin—came to be viewed as a patriarch of the ancient Koreans, scholars in the late Choson period tended to valorize him. And since his name appears explicitly in the *Yijing* (in the fifth line statement of the Mingyi hexagram ["Suppression of the Light," number 36]), some Korean scholars—including Chong Yagyong—came to believe that Jizi may have had a role in writing a portion of the basic text of the *Changes*.

Another expression of *Yijing*-related cultural pride in Korea was the production of a book by Kim Hang (Kim Il-bu, 1826–88) titled the *Correct Changes*. Kim was the teacher of a famous nationalistic Korean scholar, Sin Ch'aeho (1880–1936), who would later claim that the *Yijing* was originally a Korean text.[40] In the *Correct Changes*, Kim seeks to go beyond the accomplishments of China's early sages by devising a trigram configuration that differs from both the standard Former Heaven sequence attributed to Fuxi and the Later Heaven sequence attributed to King Wen. In this new configuration, the positions of Qian and Kun in the Former Heaven sequence are reversed (so that Kun is in the south) and Gen, the "youngest son" trigram, is in the east (where the developmental order of the Later Heaven sequence normally begins). By so doing, Kim symbolically privileges Korea as the center of a new world order for the future—heralding a new age of peace, prosperity, and joy.[41] Kim also devised a "*Correct Changes* Diagram of Metal and Fire," which served as the conceptual equivalent of China's famous Yellow River Chart and Luo River Writing.[42]

These nineteenth-century efforts in Korea to amplify the content and to change the orientation of the *Yijing* recall similar but much earlier attempts in China to go beyond the *Changes*—notably Yang Xiong's *Classic of Great Mystery* and the apocryphal Han treatise known as *Opening up the Regularities of Qian*. But Kim's approach was nationalistically inspired—a nationalism reflected in the views of many exponents of "*Changes* Studies" in Korea to this day.[43]

Vietnam

Nationalism also inspired creative scholarship on the *Yijing* in nineteenth- and twentieth-century Vietnam. But from the end of China's thousand-year occupation of north Vietnam (also known as Tonkin) in the tenth century CE until well into the French colonial era, most Vietnamese intellectuals enthusiastically embraced Chinese classical scholarship, aspiring to be part of a distinctively Sinic "domain of manifest civility"—the Vietnamese equivalent of the long-standing Chinese notion of their country as the "domain of ritual propriety and moral duty."[44]

To be sure, from at least the thirteenth century onward (and especially from the sixteenth to the nineteenth centuries), use of the unique Chu-Nom or Nom script—a complex and uniquely Vietnamese system of writing based in part on the same visual, phonetic, and semantic principles used to construct characters in classical Chinese—had the effect of making works identified with other cultural traditions (including, of course, the *Yijing*) seem somewhat more "Vietnamese." But on the whole, in Vietnam, as in Korea and Japan, the prestige of Chinese characters was so great that elites tended to write primarily in classical Chinese until the late nineteenth or early twentieth century—even though alternative, indigenously developed scripts such as Nom, Korean Hangul, and Japanese Kana had been available for hundreds of years.

The *Yijing* was probably introduced into Vietnam at about the same time as it reached Korea and Japan, but it did not become influential until the establishment of the Le dynasty (1428–1789). During that period Cheng-Zhu Neo-Confucianism became state orthodoxy, and the *Changes* was studied both as a Confucian classic at the Imperial College and as a divination manual at the Ministry of Rites. Even then, however, it did not occupy a particularly important place in the Vietnamese examination system, and few students seem to have specialized in it.[45]

Nonetheless, as in Tokugawa Japan and Choson Korea, ideas derived from the *Yijing* influenced many realms of Le dynasty culture, from politics, music, art, literature, and mathematics to medicine, agriculture, calendrical studies, geography, religion, popular lore, and a wide range of divinatory theories and practices. Moreover several Le dynasty scholars became quite famous for their writings on the *Changes*—notably Nguyen Binh Khiem (1491–1585), the preeminent Nom poet of his age and a man known popularly today as the "Vietnamese Nostradamus." Philosophically Nguyen used the *Yijing* to unite Neo-Confucian metaphysics with Daoism and Buddhism. He also gained fame as an able and insightful exponent of Shao Yong's numerological approach to divination (Nguyen's mother reportedly taught *Yijing*-related numerology), and of the time-honored Chinese fortune-telling technique called the Great One.[46] Nguyen's writings are still studied in Vietnam for their predictions of modern events.[47]

As with Japan and Korea, scholars of the *Changes* in Le dynasty Vietnam had access to standard Chinese works on the *Yijing*, such as the Ming dynasty's *Great Comprehensive Compilation of the Zhou Changes* and the Qing period's *Balanced Compendium on the Zhou Changes*. Most such works were published in Vietnam during the eighteenth and nineteenth centuries, and all reflected an orthodoxy based on Cheng-Zhu Neo-Confucianism. But despite this official orthodoxy (or perhaps because of it), other currents of thought circulated in Vietnam at the time—as in Japan and Korea—encouraging scholars to explore new interpretative ground. Significantly many Vietnamese scholars found a preimperial form of Confucianism alluring, as it seemed to speak more directly to the politics and geography of their country than did the visions of Song and post-Song dynasty thinkers, who were themselves the products of a highly developed bureaucratic state that had been at least a thousand years in the making.[48]

Le Quy Don (1726–84), however—arguably the most important Vietnamese philosopher in the eighteenth century—had no particular interest in the distant past. His writings, including a highly regarded commentary on the *Yijing* titled *An Explanation of the Classic of Changes for Different Levels*, reflected an attraction to Chinese Evidential Studies scholarship as well as, somewhat paradoxically, a deep commitment to Cheng-Zhu thought. Drawing on Chinese, Vietnamese, and Korean traditions of practical statecraft, he used the *Yijing* explicitly to promote political and social reforms.[49] He did not, however, transgress the boundaries established by Chinese scholars in the realms of either textual interpretation or domestic politics. Nor did the work of transitional scholars such as Nhu Ba Si (1759–1840).[50]

It is sometimes said that Vietnamese scholars were not as preoccupied as their Chinese counterparts with philological and metaphysical debates.[51] But based on my own perusal of dozens of *Yijing*-related handwritten manuscripts in the Hanoi National Library that were produced in the late Le period or the early Nguyen dynasty (1802–1945), it seems clear that the authors were genuinely interested in these topics, especially metaphysics. Many of these works are undated and anonymous, and some are written at least in part in Nom characters (prose, verse, or a combination of the two). They range in length from several hundred to only a few dozen pages. Some of these manuscripts adopt a question-and-answer format, while others present their *Yijing*-related information in the form of short essays. Some texts are organized topically, and a few employ an explicitly comparative approach, analyzing the *Changes* together with other Chinese classics, such as the *Classic of Poetry* and the *Spring and Autumn Annals*.[52]

The most striking feature of these and other late Le and early Nguyen manuscripts is their philosophical eclecticism. Although most of these works give lip service to the great Song dynasty Neo-Confucian thinkers Cheng Yi and Zhu Xi, quoting liberally from their respective writings on the *Changes*, many reflect a particular interest in the numerology of the Yellow River Chart and the Luo River Writing, and in practical techniques of divination. Another interesting feature of these manuscripts is the great range in their content. Some, for example, include texts derived from spirit-writing (introduced to Vietnam from China in the latter half of the eighteenth century), and some even include account books.

The Nguyen dynasty began in the early nineteenth century with a particularly staunch defense of Neo-Confucian orthodoxy, which started to erode, however, after China's defeat in the Sino-French War of 1884–85. Prior to 1885 the Vietnamese government did much to bolster the civil service examinations and to promote Confucian morality. It published Nom editions of the Chinese classics, including the *Changes*, and adopted the commentaries of Cheng Yi and Zhu Xi as the official standard for interpretations of the *Yijing* in the Vietnamese civil service examinations.

A typical example of the way Nom writing and Cheng-Zhu textual analysis came together in support of state orthodoxy can be found in a work by Dang Thai Bang (dates unknown) titled *Songs [Explicating] the Zhou Changes in National Pronunciation* (1815; see figure 4.3). This work—which includes four prefaces, a poetic inscription, and an account of milfoil divination ritual based on the model established by Zhu Xi—consists primarily of divided pages in which the basic text of the *Yijing* occupies the top of each page and a series of songs in "six-eight" verse corresponding to it appear at the bottom. The songs and commentaries consist mainly of Chinese characters interspersed with Nom characters.

For the most part, the prefaces to the work express routine opinions about the *Changes*, but they make a special point of applauding the author's decision to offer a verse interpretation in "national pronunciation" as a means of introducing novices to the *Yijing*. Take, for example, the preface written by Pham Quy Thich (1759–1825), who himself produced several im-

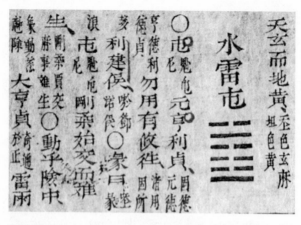

FIGURE 4.3

Vietnamese *Yijing* Manuscript in Classical Chinese and Nom
Characters

This partial page from Dang Thai Bang's *Songs [Explicating] the
Zhou Changes in National Pronunciation* depicts the Zhun
hexagram (number 3 in the conventional sequence). Above it, in
large characters, are the primary qualities of its constituent
trigrams, "Water" (Kan) above and "Thunder" (Zhen) below,
followed by the hexagram name (an unusual configuration). To
the left of these elements are the judgment and a series of
commentaries written in small Chinese and Nom characters.
Reproduced with permission from the Vietnamese Nom
Preservation Foundation and the National Library of Vietnam,
http://nomfoundation.org.

portant works on the *Changes*. Pham begins with a
discussion of how commentaries on ancient works
elucidate the ideas of the Confucian sages, noting that
without such explanations, the "meanings and principles" expressed by the sages cannot be fully understood. He goes on to emphasize the difficulty of the

document (which he describes as more subtle and profound than any other book), Dang's deep familiarity with the classic, and the need to instruct Vietnamese students using the national pronunciation. Pham points out that although the classical learning of the Vietnamese and the Chinese is the same, Vietnamese pronunciations of the written characters are different—thus the need to create a version of the classic that is both accessible to Vietnamese students and easy to learn through chanting.

The writings of the great nineteenth-century scholar Nguyen Khuyen (1835–1909) place in sharp relief the tensions created by Western imperialism, particularly after 1885. They reveal a sharp critique of Vietnamese society under French colonial rule as well as Nguyen's anguish over not being able to alter the situation. Here is an undated poem by Nguyen in classical Chinese that captures his emotions:

> How can a winter day compete in length with a
>   summer one?
> [Yet] the south breeze is as cool as the north wind.
> Thinking [that a rotten rat is] tasty, the owl scolds
>   the phoenix;
> A cunning mind is never exhausted, as the oriole
>   catches the cicada.
> If the realm within the oceans opens up to a new
>   world
> People's customs should join [reflect] the pristine
>   vastness of the ancient past.

Up alone in the early morning, I study the *Changes*
[But] the increase and decrease [of the current sit-
uation] are hard to discern.[53]

Here, with allusions to the ruminations of the Tang
calligrapher Liu Gongquan (778–865) about the
length of days in winter and summer and two parables
from the Daoist philosopher Zhuangzi (the story of a
"tasty" rotten rat and the tale of a bird who is after a
mantis who is after a cicada—all of whom are captured
by a hunter), Nguyen expresses his anxiety and uncer-
tainty about the present and the future. The *Changes*
in this context provides no solace.

Although by the late Nguyen period Chinese-style
Confucian scholarship in Vietnam was in decline and
under pressure, at least a few classically trained and nationalistically minded Vietnamese scholars tried to use
the *Changes* and other Chinese works to advocate reform. One such person was Le Van Ngu (b. 1859), an
examination failure who traveled to Europe for three
months in 1900 and came back radicalized.[54] Le considered himself to be a "wild scholar"—a maverick
who dared to criticize Zhu Xi and other exponents of
"orthodox studies" in Vietnam. But he was also critical
of Han and Tang scholarship on the *Changes* and had
no use at all for post-Song scholarship on the classic. In
this sense he was very much like the Korean scholar
Chong Yagyong, who became highly critical of almost
all major Chinese commentaries on the *Yijing*. In the
preface to one of his most famous writings, Le tells us:

"Born thousands of years [after the sages] and having witnessed the decline of *Changes* scholarship and the rise of heretical views, I have been engrossed in the study of the *Yijing*. I have discovered ideas undiscovered by former Confucians and elaborated ideas not yet fully elaborated."[55]

Like the Chinese scholars Fang Yizhi and Jiang Yong at an earlier time, Le held the Yellow River Chart and the Luo River Writing in especially high regard, believing that "all natural principles" could be found in these two numerological illustrations. He did not, however, admire the *Yijing*-related speculations of Shao Yong, whose ideas seemed too complicated and abstract.

Perhaps the most interesting aspect of Le's thought is the way he used the *Changes* to interpret various Western-inspired ideas, from science and technology to politics and theology. Convinced that an enthusiasm for Western learning among the Vietnamese people had led them to decadence, materialism, selfishness, and a general neglect of the hallowed *Yijing*, he argued that the slavish embrace of Western civilization would only bring more difficulties and suffering to his people. Although he valued the political principle of constitutional monarchy and used an analysis of the Bo hexagram ("Peeling," number 23) to justify it, he was far less taken with Western science, maintaining that the wonders of the *Changes* were "ten thousand times more amazing than the Western principles of cannon, ships, cars, and electricity."[56]

Tibet

The history of both the transmission and the use of the *Yijing* in Tibet offers a striking contrast to that in Vietnam, Korea, and Japan. First, unlike the elites in the latter three East Asian countries, comparatively few Tibetan scholars knew any classical Chinese. Second, Indian influence was far stronger in Tibet than it was in these other areas, which were all well within the Chinese cultural orbit.

The *Yijing* initially came to Tibet as a respected Chinese classic during the early Tang dynasty, in the seventh century CE, but it seems to have never acquired the aura there that attached to it in most of East Asia. Nor did it permeate many realms of Tibetan culture, as it did in Japan, Korea, and Vietnam. To be sure, by late Tang times Tibetan diviners had begun to use the trigrams of the *Changes* in more or less the Chinese fashion, and later they also borrowed some of the numerological diagrams of the *Yijing*—notably the Luo River Writing—known popularly as the "Nine Palaces."

But the Tibetans seem not to have made much use of hexagrams for divinatory or other symbolic purposes, and although some Tibetan lamas, such as Thuken Losang Chokyi Nyima (also known as Thu'u-bkwan blo-bzan-chos-kyi-ni-ma, 1737–1802), had a scholarly interest in the *Changes*, reliable information on the nature of their work is difficult to come by.[57] We do know, however, that Thuken, who reportedly studied at the Tibetan Buddhist Yonghe Temple in Beijing for three years, wrote a famous study of Asian philosophical thought titled *The Crystal Mirror of Philosophical Systems*, which devotes at least some attention to the history of the *Yijing*, the Luo River Writing, and related Chinese divination texts.[58]

For at least a thousand years there have been three main types of Tibetan divination, in addition to various techniques associated with the indigenous Bon tradition: (1) Astrology, (2) a rare and secret approach called Martial Conquest, and (3) Elemental Divination. In popular usage the Tibetan divinatory arts tend to be identified either with India-based "White Calculations," named after the Tibetan term for India, or China-based "Black Calculations," named after the Tibetan word for China. Fundamentally, Chinese-style Elemental Divination, and more recent forms of divination and astrology that were introduced into Tibet from China during the mid-seventeenth century, are viewed as a Black Calculations.

In Black Calculations, which have been influenced by each of China's "Three Teachings" (Confucianism, Daoism, and Buddhism), we find a concern with many of the cosmic variables that are characteristic of *Changes* interpretations throughout East Asia: yin and yang (the Tibetan equivalents are *pho* and *mo*), calendrical cycles of twelve and sixty, the five agents, the eight trigrams, and "magic squares" (known generically in Tibetan as *mewa* and in Mongolian as *mangga*), based on the numerical configurations of the Luo

River Writing.[59] Tibetan tradition traces Elemental Divination to Fuxi, the putative inventor of the eight trigrams in China; hence their importance in this system. Many of the other symbols in Tibetan divination are entirely domestic in origin or at least have no discernible Chinese roots.

The famous late-eighteenth-century work by Sangye Gyatso (also rendered as Sangs-rgyas rGya-mtsho, 1653–1705)—known popularly as the *White Beryl Treatise*—shows, with the aid of strikingly beautiful illustrations, how trigrams, magic squares, and the five agents from the Chinese tradition, together with the symbols of the Indian zodiac, interact to shed light on the future.[60] Gyurme Dorje's introduction to the *White Beryl Treatise* describes the elaborate preparations and ceremonies that accompany a formal divination. First, he says, "dreams should be inspected and recognized as auspicious or inauspicious, according to the criteria in the *White Beryl*." Other preparations focus on the specific time and place of the divination. In general, prognostications "should be carried out during the waxing phase of the lunar month"—in the morning to determine past signs, in the afternoon to determine future signs, and around noon to determine present events. Food or incense should be offered to the local deities. In all these activities, both the diviner and the subject should pay homage to the various Buddhas as well as to the lineage-holders of elemental divination, and all the particular deities associated with the directions, animal signs, agents, trigrams, numeric squares, planets, and constellations, "inviting them to be present, conjoined with offering prayers and confession prayers."[61]

The divination itself involves the use of black, neutral, or mottled pebbles to represent the various relationships existing among the five agents, trigrams, numbered squares, and animal signs. After arranging these pebbles (or employing an analogous chart), the diviner makes a determination according to the stipulations of the *White Beryl Treatise*.[62] Gyurme Dorje concludes his description with the following explanation: "Lying at the heart of all these [divinatory] understandings is the notion of 'auspicious coincidence' (*rten-'brel*). From the Buddhist point of view, the term *rten-'brel* refers to the twelve links of dependent origination (*pratityasamutpada*), through which past actions bring about present and future results within the course of cyclic existence." He goes on to say that "it is important to bear in mind that the predictions are not considered to be deterministic, but cautionary and prescriptive. If the outcome is auspicious, no action need be taken, but if the portents are negative, the subject is strongly advised to undertake the appropriate counteracting rites which have the power to nullify those negative influences."[63]

As these remarks clearly indicate, all Tibetan divinatory systems are based on Buddhist assumptions about the world of "conventional reality" rather than "ultimate reality." They do not conflict with Buddhist notions of karmic retribution, for even when one's lifespan seems to be determined by one or another divinatory technique, the length of that life, like other aspects of the future, depends on which of its various karmas (i.e., thoughts and deeds) "ripen." Thus, although a divination or horoscope analysis can provide a general prediction of the situations that might be encountered in one's life, there are no assurances that the life in question will actually unfold in any particular way. In a sense, then, the assumptions of Tibetan divination are like those of the *Yijing*: certain circumstances will naturally occur in the course of a life, but how one responds to them will ultimately determine the outcome.

In traditional Tibetan society, astrologers might be lamas, monks, or specially trained laypersons who received donations from the public for their demonstrable divinatory (and often medical) skills.[64] In large monasteries monks determined auspicious times for Buddhist ceremonies, made forecasts for weather and harvests, and compiled calendars and almanacs for a variety of religious events and holidays. These almanacs often shared features with those of the Chinese, Japanese, Koreans, and Vietnamese, including a preoccupation with lucky and unlucky days for various activities.[65] In rural Tibet local specialists divined for villagers, casting horoscopes for newborn children, comparing astrological profiles for couples contemplating wedlock, predicting auspicious geomantic sites for buildings and graves, and determining appropriate

FIGURE 4.4
Trigrams on a Tibetan Ritual Horn
Photo taken by author.

times for weddings, funerals, and other occasions. The charts that informed such predictions were ubiquitous in premodern Tibet and have been described and illustrated in a great many publications.[66]

Like other peoples in East Asia, the Tibetans seem to have been eager to domesticate the *Yijing*—that is, to assimilate it to their indigenous culture. Some Tibetan commentators in the past have emphasized affinities between the *Changes* and Tantric Buddhism, and other scholars in both the Buddhist and Bon traditions have transformed Confucius—the putative transmitter of *Yijing* divination (and other forms of fortune-telling, according to Tibetan tradition)—into their own religious figure, named Kong-tse 'phrulr-gyal or Khong-spu-rtsi, an emanation of Manjugh-osa, one of many forms assumed by the bodhisattva Manjushri.[67]

As another example of this process of domestica-tion, in Tibet the eight trigrams sometimes acquired symbolic identifications that were very different from their traditional Chinese ones. Zhen, for example, usually associated with thunder, came to be linked in certain Tibetan divination systems with "meteoric iron."[68] And when displayed as protective symbols on various craft productions, including woodblock prints and the bright silk Tibetan paintings known as thang-kas, the eight trigrams often appear in configurations other than the standard Former Heaven (Fuxi) and Later Heaven (King Wen) sequences of the Chinese tradition. At times in these varied Tibetan configura-tions, certain trigrams are repeated while others are omitted.[69]

There are other significant differences between Chi-nese and Tibetan divinatory symbolism. For instance the five agents and the twelve zodiacal animals of Tibet do not always correspond exactly to their Chinese counterparts (this is true also of the Vietnamese zo-diac). Similarly correlations between the eight trigrams and the five agents in Tibet do not always conform to Chinese models. In fact, in some Tibetan cosmological constructions, each trigram has a different agent associ-ated with it, requiring the addition of non-Chinese agents such as air.[70] Moreover the Tibetans created new divinatory symbols, including four-lined tetragrams—although there was, of course, a Chinese precedent for this sort of representation with Yang Xiong's well-known *Classic of Great Mystery*.[71]

The *Yijing* in Modern East Asia

During the late nineteenth and early twentieth centuries, imperialism became an increasingly prominent theme in the histories of the four cultures mentioned above. But foreign aggression in East Asia played itself out in very different ways. China, first to feel the sting of Western imperialism, suffered under the yoke of the infamous "unequal treaties" from 1842 to 1943. Japan, subject to a similar set of onerous stipulations beginning in the 1850s, became an imperialist power itself after the Meiji Restoration of 1868, colonizing Taiwan in 1895 and then Korea in 1910. Vietnam fell increasingly under French domination in the late nineteenth and early twentieth centuries, only to be subjugated by the Japanese in 1940. Tibet, initially threatened by the British, became more or less independent from 1912 to 1950, but the Chinese periodically attempted to exert what they considered to be suzerain control over Tibet.

Under these circumstances traditional attitudes began to break down. Nonetheless, as we have seen in the cases of China, Korea, and Vietnam, the study and use of the *Yijing* continued in certain circles during the early twentieth century. The same was true in Japan.

Indeed, divination with the *Changes*, particularly as practiced by an entrepreneur named Takashima Kaemon (1832–1914), was a significant theme in the political history of Meiji Japan. Consulted by a great many bureaucrats throughout the Meiji period (1868–1912), Takashima became hugely popular as both a scholar and a diviner, not only in Japan but also in China, where a Chinese edition of his famous book *My Judgment on the Changes* circulated among Qing dynasty scholars and officials. One of his followers, Sugiura Shigetake (1855–1924), also translated the book into English.[72]

Remarkable transformations have taken place in the political, social, and cultural environments of Japan, Korea, and Vietnam during the post–World War II era, but nothing has been as dramatic in any of these areas as the "*Yijing* fever" that swept over China during the 1980s and 1990s. This enthusiasm for the classic had both a popular and an academic dimension, and it was manifest in an avalanche of books and journals of every conceivable sort. Nor, as far as I know, has there been anything in the rest of East Asia like the establishment of the *Zhouyi* Theme Park (in Fuling, Sichuan), a vast complex marking the spot where, nearly a thousand years ago, the Song scholar Cheng Yi, in banishment, completed his famous commentary on the *Changes*.[73] Although *Yijing*-based divinatory practices continue to be discouraged by communist governments, professional diviners can easily be found in

China and Vietnam (although not, as far as I know, in North Korea).

There has been one *Yijing*-related development outside of China worthy of at least brief mention: the establishment in 1926 in Vietnam of the highly eclectic transnational Cao Dai religion, which boasts an estimated several million adherents. The supreme deity or "God" of the Cao Dai faith is an amalgamation of Buddhist, Daoist, and Confucian cosmogonic and cosmological concepts. The Cao Dai story of creation, in brief, is that the eternal Dao generated a "father-mother" God, who created yin and yang, which in turn produced all things. In 1920 God revealed the Cao Dai teachings to Ngo Van Chieu (1878–1932?), a Vietnamese administrator, and then to others through the medium of spirit-writing. The structure of the church is fundamentally Catholic; the ethics are overwhelmingly Confucian, and the symbolism includes elements from the *Yijing*, notably dragons and trigrams (albeit unusually arranged).[74] Among the deities of this religion are the Buddha, Confucius, Jesus, and Laozi; its three primary saints are Sun Yat-sen (1866–1925; Chinese revolutionary and political leader), Victor Hugo (1802–85; French writer, artist, and statesman), and Nguyen Binh Khiem (1491–1585; Vietnamese administrator, educator, and poet). One of the three administrative branches of the Cao Dai teaching is the Eight Trigrams Palace, which "directs all activities of the universe under the leadership of God and [the] Holy Spirits."[75]

The Westward Travels of the *Changes*

CHAPTER 5

In several respects the transmission of the *Changes* to the West parallels the process by which Buddhism and Daoism traveled to Europe and the Americas. In each case Western "missionaries" played a part in the process, and in each case there were varied responses over time, ranging from blind indifference to rational knowledge, romantic fantasy, and existential engagement.[1] But in nearly every instance, as in East Asia, there was an effort, often quite self-conscious, to assimilate and domesticate the classic. As with the Koreans, Japanese, Vietnamese, and Tibetans, Westerners sent missions to China, and they brought back all kinds of useful information. But compared to their East Asian counterparts, these Western missions proceeded from very different motives and had a very different focus. Moreover, in contrast to the premodern spread of the *Yijing* and other texts to Japan, Korea, and Vietnam, where elites were completely comfortable with the classical Chinese script, in the West the *Changes* required translation, raising issues of commensurability and incommensurability that are still hotly debated today.[2]

The Jesuits and the *Changes*

Ironically the westward movement of the *Yijing* began with the eastward movement of the West. Beginning in the late sixteenth century, in a pattern replicated in many other parts of the world, Jesuit missionaries traveled to China, attempting to assimilate themselves as much as possible to the host country. They studied the Chinese language, learned Chinese customs, and sought to understand China's philosophical and religious traditions—all with the goal of winning converts by underscoring affinities between the Bible and the Confucian classics. Naturally the *Changes* served as a major focus for their proselytizing scholarship.[3]

The Jesuit missionaries labored under a double burden. Their primary duty was to bring Christianity to China (and to other parts of the world), but they also had to justify their evangelical methods to their colleagues and superiors in Europe. A kind of "double domestication" thus took place. In China the Jesuits had to make the Bible appear familiar to the Chinese, while in Europe they had to make Chinese works such as the *Yijing* appear familiar (or at least reasonable) to Europeans.

One of the primary agents involved in this process was the French Jesuit Joachim Bouvet (1656–1730), who tutored the great Kangxi emperor for up to two hours a day in algebra and geometry. In addition the two men regularly discussed the *Yijing*, which fascinated both of them. The emperor, who considered

Bouvet perhaps the only Westerner who was "really conversant with Chinese literature," showed a particular interest in the Jesuit priest's claim to be able to predict the future, including the duration of the world, with numerological charts based on the *Changes*.[4]

Bouvet and his colleague Jean-François Fouquet (1665–1741) represented a development in Western Christianity known as the Figurist movement. In brief, the Figurists tried to find in the Old Testament evidence of the coming and significance of Christ through an analysis of "letters, words, persons, and events." Apart from the literal meaning of the "outer" text, in other words, there existed a hidden "inner" meaning to be discovered. In China this gave rise to a concerted effort to find reflections (that is, "figures") of the biblical patriarchs and examples of biblical revelation in the Chinese classics themselves.

Bouvet and Fouquet were masters of the Figurist art form. Using a rather strained etymological approach to various written texts, as well as an evaluation of the trigrams and hexagrams of the *Yijing*, they found all kinds of hidden messages. Dissection of the Chinese character for Heaven (天) into the number two (二) and the word for Man (人) indicated a prophecy of the second Adam, Jesus Christ. The character for boat (船) could be broken down conveniently into the semantic indicator for a "vessel that travels on water" (舟) and the characters for "eight" (八) and "mouth(s)" (口)—signifying China's early awareness of Noah's

Ark, which contained, of course, the eight members of Noah's family.

In Figurist discourse a wide variety of Chinese philosophical terms closely associated with the *Changes* came to be equated with the Christian conception of God, including not only Heaven and the Lord on High, but also the Supreme Ultimate, the Supreme One, the Way, Principle, and even yin and yang. In the Figurist view the three solid lines of the Qian trigram ("Heaven," number 1) represented an early awareness of the Trinity; the hexagram Xu ("Waiting," number 5), with its stark reference to "clouds rising up to Heaven" (in the Commentary on the Images), indicated "the glorious ascent of the Savior"; and, of course, the Qian hexagram (number 1) referred to Creation itself. The hexagrams Pi ("Obstruction," number 12) and Tai ("Peace," number 11) referred, respectively, to "the world corrupted by sin" and "the world restored by the Incarnation," and so forth.

In focusing his attention primarily on the imagery, allusions, and numerology of the *Yijing*, Bouvet was following a path blazed by Chinese Christian writers such as the late Ming convert Shao Fuzhong (fl. 1596), whose book, *On the Heavenly Learning*, draws on the Great Commentary, hexagram analysis, and the writings of Shao Yong and others in comparing concepts and images in the *Yijing* with various Catholic doctrines such as the Trinity and the Immaculate Conception. Other Chinese converts wrote similar tracts identifying affinities between Catholic theology and the *Changes*.

One of Bouvet's greatest and most persistent desires was to demonstrate a relationship between the numbers and diagrams of the *Yijing* (especially as expressed in the Yellow River Chart and the Luo River Writing) and the systems of Pythagoras, the neo-Platonists, and the kabbala. This is evident not only in his Chinese-language writings, but also in his broad-ranging manuscripts in Latin. In one such manuscript, for example, he equates the Ain Soph (sometimes translated as "Limitless Divine Creator") symbol at the top of the Ten Sephiroth (the so-called Tree of Life) with the Diagram of the Supreme Ultimate, remarking that the ancient Chinese sages understood the doctrine of "the one and triune God, founder of all things, . . . [as well as] the incarnation of the Son of God and the reformation of the world through him." This understanding, Bouvet asserts, was "clearly similar to the ancient kabbala of the Hebrews," whether expressed by the "ten elementary numbers and the twenty-two letters of its mystic alphabet," or by the twenty-two Chinese characters representing the ten heavenly stems and twelve earthly branches as well as the "ten elementary numbers of the mystic figure *Ho tu* [Yellow River Chart]."[5]

Bouvet goes on to argue in this tract that the first two hexagrams of the *Yijing*, Qian and Kun, are the "principal characters of God [as] creator and redeemer." Qian, "with the numerical power 216, the triple of the tetra-gram number 72, is the symbol of justice," and Kun, "with the numerical power 144, double the number 72, is the symbol of mercy." Together, "taken up with the power of the same tetragram number 72 quintupled, [these numbers] are the symbolic mark of the two principal virtues of the divine Redeemer, outlined in the hieroglyphics of the Chinese just as in the sephirotic system of the Hebrews." In short, Bouvet concludes, because God "made everything in number, weight, and measure (Sap. XI, 21), . . . perfecting these in wisdom," it follows, "by necessity, that the numbers are, so to speak, the fundamental base of all true philosophy, . . . the sacred wisdom of the old patriarchs . . . infused in the very first-formed parent of human beings."[6]

Bouvet's "Chart of Heavenly Superiority and Earthly Subordination" represents his effort to integrate the numerology of the Yellow River Chart and the Luo River Writing into a single mathematical "grand synthesis," similar in certain respects to Shao Yong's Former Heaven Chart. Like Shao's diagram, but with less schematic economy, the Chart of Heavenly Superiority and Earthly Subordination attempts to convey "the quintessence of heavenly patterns and earthly configurations," illustrating not only the evolution of but also the mutual interaction between the hexagrams and their constituent trigrams and lines. And like Shao Yong's numerical calculations, Bouvet's diagrams were designed to yield an understanding of good and bad fortune as well as an appreciation of the larger patterns of cosmic regularity and cosmic change (see figure 5.1).[7]

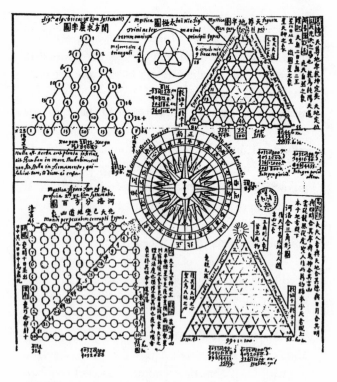

FIGURE 5.1

One Version of Bouvet's Chart of Heavenly Superiority and
Earthly Subordination

This diagram, one of many such illustrations produced by Bouvet
and contained in the Vatican Archives as well as in other libraries
(the chart depicted here is from the Bibliothèque nationale in
France), is based on geometric figures of the sort displayed in
figure 3.6. The chart seeks to show the patterns of cosmic change
that will lead ultimately to the "Second Coming of Christ."
Originally published in Claudia von Collani's *Joachim Bouvet S.J.:
Sein Leben und Sein Werk*, *Monumenta Serica*, Monograph Series
17 (Steyler Verlag, 1985), 169. Reproduced with permission from
Monumenta Serica.

Initially the Kangxi emperor's interest in Bouvet's ideas was so great that he encouraged the French Jesuit to play an active role in the compilation of the huge annotated edition of the *Yijing* that was published in 1715 as the *Balanced Compendium on the Zhou Changes*— which Bouvet indeed did. But eventually the Figurist enterprise, like the broader Jesuit evangelical movement, fell victim to harsh criticisms from Chinese scholars as well as to vigorous attacks by other members of the Christian community in China and abroad. In the end Rome proscribed all Bouvet's Figurist writings and forbade him to promulgate his Figurist ideas among the Chinese.[8]

Yet despite the unhappy fate of the Figurists in China, their writings captured the attention of several prominent European intellectuals in the late seventeenth and early eighteenth centuries—most notably the great German philosopher and mathematician Gottfried Wilhelm Leibniz (1646–1716).[9] Leibniz's interest in China had been provoked by, among other things, his search for a "Primitive Language"—one that existed before the Flood. Both Bouvet and Leibniz believed that the study of the *Changes* could assist in this quest, and in the creation of a comprehensive scientific/mathematical language that Leibniz referred to as the "Universal Characteristic." Such a language would make the act of thinking—like the act of calculation—a reflection of the binary structure of nature itself. In their view Shao Yong's Former Heaven Chart (figure 5.2) offered a mathematical point of entry: a

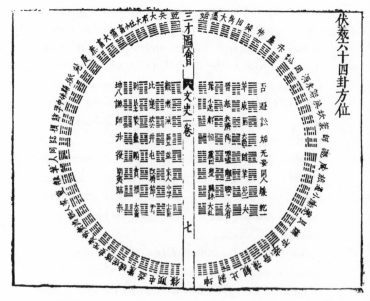

FIGURE 5.2
Shao Yong's Former Heaven Chart
These circular and square configurations of the sixty-four
hexagrams show a progression of line changes that suggested an
obvious binary mathematical structure to Bouvet and Leibniz.

hexagram structure of line changes that expressed exactly the same formal features as the binary system invented by Leibniz himself.

When Bouvet sent a copy of Shao Yong's diagram to
Leibniz, the latter was ecstatic to see cross-cultural con-
firmation of his binary system—a system that had a religious and mystical significance to both of them, denoting the idea that God (represented by the number
one) had created everything out of nothing (o).[10] But

while there are indeed certain similarities between the ideas and approaches of Leibniz and Shao Yong, there are also significant differences. First, the numbers Shao Yong employed in all his calculations were based on the decimal system, as were those of every other commentator on the *Changes* up to the time of Bouvet. Second, Shao was clearly more interested in correlative metaphysical explanations and analogies between natural bodies and processes than in the binary structure of the Former Heaven Chart per se. On the whole Shao had little interest in quantitative and empirical methods, and he did not share Leibniz's optimistic belief in linear progress. To Shao all experience was cyclical, and empirical study was merely a technical exercise, like the practice of astronomy or divination.[11]

Thus, in a sense, the Bouvet-Leibniz exchange serves as a metaphor for the problems facing exponents of a Chinese-Christian synthesis in both China and Europe. Provocative similarities could be identified but not fully exploited, not least because people like Bouvet faced such formidable opposition within the Catholic Church, both from other orders (Franciscans and Dominicans) and from within the Jesuit community itself. Meanwhile, in European secular society, individuals such as Voltaire, who idealized Chinese culture for his own ideological purposes, criticized Leibniz unmercifully for his Panglossian optimism. Thus knowledge continued to be acquired about China, but in a piecemeal fashion, and by the early nineteenth century it came with an increasingly negative spin.

Translating the *Changes*

The first book in a European language to give substantial attention to the *Changes* was a Jesuit compilation known as *Confucius Sinarum Philosophus* (Confucius, Philosopher of the Chinese; 1687). Although acknowledging that the *Yijing* had been "misused" by Daoist fortune-tellers and "atheists" (i.e., Neo-Confucians), it chronicled the generally accepted history of the document, emphasizing the moral content of the work. Like many Chinese Christians who sought to use the symbols of the *Changes* to illustrate biblical virtues, the editors of *Confucius Sinarum Philosophus* focused on the Qian hexagram ("Modesty," number 15). Following the gloss of a famous Ming dynasty scholar, they pointed out that the lower Gen trigram signifies a mountain rising from the depths of the earth up to the clouds and the stars—a symbol of sublimity and great virtue. The foundations of the mountain lie in the upper trigram, Kun, which signifies Earth—the symbol of modesty with its hidden treasures, bearing fruit for all humankind.[12]

Significantly the first complete translation of the *Changes* in a Western language (Latin) was undertaken by three Jesuit scholars who were extremely critical of the allegorical approach adopted by Bouvet and his followers. This anti-Figurist group consisted of Jean-Baptiste Regis (1663–1738), Pierre-Vincent de Tartre (1669–1724), and Joseph Marie Anne de Moyriac de Mailla (1669–1748). All three men denied that the

Chinese classics contained any truths of the Christian faith, and they all denounced the Figurists for producing what de Tartre disparagingly called the "Cabala [Kabbala] of the Enochists."[13]

Work began on the translation in 1707, but the preliminary draft was not completed until 1723.[14] This final version was based on the imperially commissioned *Balanced Compendium on the Zhou Changes* and its official Manchu rendering. But the Regis manuscript then languished for more than a decade in Paris, until a young sinologist named Julius Mohl (1800–1876) produced a two-volume printed version of several hundred pages in the 1830s titled *Y-King antiquissimus Sinarum liber quem ex latina interpretatione P. Regis aliorumque ex Soc Jesu P.P. edidit Julius Mohl* (*Yijing*, the Most Ancient Book of the Chinese, Edited by Julius Mohl Based on the Latin translation of Father Regis and Other Fathers of the Society of Jesus). This version, which drew on other materials in addition to the Regis manuscript, attacked the Figurists as well as the theories of Shao Yong. At the same time, however, in a series of introductory essays, dissertations, and appendices, it addressed most of the major issues of traditional Chinese *Yijing* scholarship in a systematic way, quoting from orthodox Neo-Confucian sources and citing the authority of the Church fathers and Western philosophers for comparative purposes.[15]

During the latter part of the nineteenth century, after a long hiatus, a flurry of translations of the *Changes* appeared in Europe, including Canon Thomas Mc-Clatchie's *A Translation of the Confucian Yi-king* (1876); Angelo Zottoli's 1880 rendering in volume 3 of his *Cursus Litteraturae Sinicae neo-missionariis accomodatus* (Course of Chinese Literature Appropriate for New Missionaries; 1879–82); James Legge's *The Yi King* (1882); Paul-Louis-Felix Philastre's *Tscheou Yi* (1885–93); and Charles de Harlez's *Le Yih-king: Texte primitif, retabli, traduit et commente* (1889).[16] These works reflect a "scholarly vogue in European culture at this time concerned with the uncovering, and the rational and historical explanation, of all manner of apparent Oriental mysteries," including not only Buddhism and Daoism, but also various forms of spiritualism—notably Theosophy, an eclectic, Asian-oriented belief system focused on self-realization and "oneness with the Divine," which some have seen as a precursor to the so-called New Age Movement of the 1980s in Europe and the United States.[17]

Zottoli's incomplete and undistinguished translation appears to have had a rather limited circulation in Europe, but the renderings by Philastre, a naval officer, diplomat, and teacher, and de Harlez, a Belgian priest and professor, were somewhat more popular, at least in France.[18] Both publications have serious limitations as scholarly works, but each is at least comparatively lively and easy to read. Philastre's problem as a translator is that his renderings are rather loose; the difficulty with de Harlez is that his approach to the *Changes* is highly idiosyncratic, predicated on the idea that the classic began as a reference book for some unnamed ancient Chinese political figure.[19]

McClatchie, like Father Joachim Bouvet before him, maintained that the *Yijing* had been carried to China by one of the sons of Noah after the Deluge. But whereas Bouvet had tried to use the *Changes* to prove that the ancient Chinese had knowledge of the "one true God," McClatchie believed that the work reflected a form of pagan materialism, "perfected by Nimrod and his Cushites before the dispersion from Babel." He identified Shangdi (the ancient Shang dynasty deity) as the Baal of the Chaldeans and pointed to a number of cross-cultural correlations involving the number eight, including the total number of Noah's family, the principal gods of the Egyptians, and the major manifestations of the Hindu deity Shiva.[20]

In addition to offering a relatively straightforward, but not very illuminating, translation of the *Changes*, McClatchie published two articles in the *China Review* at about the same time—one titled "The Symbols of the *Yih-King*" and the other, "Phallic Worship." In these two works, particularly the latter, he identified the first two hexagrams of the *Yijing* with the male and female sexual organs, respectively. In McClatchie's view Qian and Kun represented the "phallic God of Heathendom." Qian "or his Male portion is the membrum virile," and Kun "or his Female portion is the pudendum muliebre." These two, he goes on to say, "are enclosed in the circle or ring, or phallus," known as the Supreme Ultimate or Great One, from which "all things are generated."[21] Scholars like Legge and, later, the eminent Russian Sinologist Iulian Shchutskii ridiculed this decidedly sexual view (Shchutskii described it as the product of "pseudoscientific delirium"), but recent work by other scholars suggests its essential validity.[22]

James Legge began his translation of the *Changes* in 1854, with the later assistance of a Chinese scholar, Wang Tao (1828–97). But for various reasons it was not completed for another twenty years or so.[23] Like the Jesuits Legge believed that the Confucian classics were compatible with Christian beliefs, but he was not a Figurist.[24] In addition to denouncing McClatchie for focusing on the *Yijing*'s sexual imagery, Legge assailed him for resorting to the methods of "Comparative Mythology." In Legge's dismissive words, "I have followed Canon McClatchie's translation from paragraph to paragraph and from sentence to sentence, but found nothing which I could employ with advantage in my own."[25]

Legge had no love of China and no respect for the *Yijing*. Indeed, he described it as "a farrago of emblematic representations." Although admitting that the *Changes* was "an important monument of architecture," he characterized it as "very bizarre in its conception and execution."[26] Legge's highly literal translation followed the prevailing Neo-Confucian orthodoxy of the Qing dynasty as reflected in the *Balanced Compendium on the Zhou Changes*. His goal was to produce a translation that made it possible for him to downplay aspects of the *Yijing* he deemed unimportant, such as its imagery and numerology, and to underscore themes he considered essential—not least the obviously mistaken idea that passages in the Explaining the Trigrams commentary refer to the Judeo-Christian God.[27]

Although Legge's translation remained the standard English-language version of the *Changes* until the mid-twentieth century, it provoked a barrage of criticism, beginning with Thomas Kingsmill in 1882. Writing in the *China Review*, Kingsmill acknowledged that Legge's rendering was somewhat better than the flawed translations of Regis, Zottoli, and McClatchie, but he faulted the Scottish Sinologue for introducing yet another system of "transcribing Chinese," and for using too many interpolated words. Kingsmill wrote: "If the translator be at liberty to introduce, even within brackets, matters altogether outside the text, there is no possibility of predicting the result, and, as in this case, an author's plain words may be made to bear any meaning at the fancy of the manipulator."[28]

Soon thereafter Joseph Edkins, a British Protestant missionary who had already spent more than twenty of his fifty-seven years in China, wrote a pair of articles on the *Yijing* that displayed a striking sensitivity to Chinese scholarship and a remarkable lack of ethnocentric prejudice. Of particular note was his emphasis on the commentaries of the Qing scholar Mao Qiling, and especially Mao's critique of Song dynasty scholars such as Chen Tuan and Shao Yong. Edkins appreciated the contributions of certain Western scholars, including Legge, but he had none of the latter's cultural prejudices. Instead he took the *Changes* on its own terms, as a reflection of the time in which it was created. It is worthwhile, he wisely concluded, "to study the opinions of the wise in all ages."[29]

At about the same time (1882–83), but with a far different intellectual orientation from that of Edkins, Albert Étienne Terrien de LaCouperie, a French scholar, wrote a long article that in 1892 became a short volume, *The Oldest Book of the Chinese: The Yh-King and Its Authors*. Terrien's study begins with a general discussion of the origin and evolution of the *Changes*, based primarily on traditional Chinese scholarship. It then evaluates "Native Interpretations" and "European Interpretations" of the *Yijing*. Although Terrien's list of Chinese commentators is relatively comprehensive, his opinion of their work is low (the product of what he derisively describes as "tortured minds" and "maddened brains"). Their approach to analyzing the text is, he claims, "undeserving the attention of a man of common sense; it is a compilation of guesses and suggestions, a monument of nonsense." He states scornfully that there are many educated Chinese who believe that "electricity, steam-power, astronomical laws, [the] sphericity of the earth, etc., are all ... to be found in the *Yh-King*."[30] This belief, as we have seen and shall see again, was commonly held but fundamentally ill-founded.

Terrien had a low opinion of most French, German, Italian, and British scholarship on the *Changes*. He does praise Zottoli for not translating the text "according to the farcical treatment of many Chinese commentators," and for "refusing to translate what cannot be translated," but he describes the Regis translation as "unsatisfactory and utterly unintelligible" and dismisses the McClatchie version as simply a reflection of the author's preconceived notions, translated "accordingly with Chinese commentators." Of Philastre's "mystical" rendering, he notes that the "symbolism of astronomy, electricity, chemistry, etc." of the *Changes* is "carried to the extreme," and that the speculations of the translator have "no other ground than the imagination of the writer."[31] As to Legge's translation of the *Yijing*, Terrien describes it as an "unintelligible" English paraphrase of the document, based solely on a "guess-at-the-meaning principle," "the most obnoxious system ever found in philology."[32]

Like Bouvet and his supporters, Terrien sought to locate the origins of the *Changes* in the West (Central Asia, to be more precise), but his intent was not to domesticate the *Yijing* in the fashion of the Figurists for he held the conventional text in very low regard. According to Terrien, the *Changes* originated as a primitive reference work—a "handbook of state management . . . set forth under the sixty-four words [hexagram names]"—in the ancient kingdom of Akkad, which he believed to be Bactria. By his account, following a great flood, the Bak people migrated eastward to China, having previously struggled with the descendants of the Assyrian king Sargon (i.e., Shennong, successor to

Fuxi). He goes on to assert that Prince Hu-Nak-kunte (Yu, founder of the Xia dynasty) then led the Bak people to settle in the Yellow River valley around the year 2282 BCE.[33]

Iulian Shchutskii's critique of Terrien is as devastating as Terrien's critique of his predecessors. Shchutskii writes, for example, that Terrien does "savage violence" to the text of the *Changes* and "completely dismisses the commentary tradition," quoting only "the most ancient layer" of the basic text and placing it "in the Procrustean bed of his own arbitrariness."[34] Legge's translation of the *Yijing* fares a bit better, but, somewhat ironically in the light of the criticisms of Terrien, Shchutskii faults the British missionary for relying too heavily on Chinese commentaries.

None of these early translations of the *Yijing* enjoyed much popularity in the late nineteenth century. Although the period witnessed a certain vogue for occult writings in Europe, the *Changes* was simply too obscure to appeal to a broader public readership. During the 1920s, however, the situation began to change dramatically. In 1924 the missionary-scholar Richard Wilhelm (1873–1930) published a German translation of the *Changes* titled *I Ging, Das Buch der Wandlungen*, which became a global sensation when it was translated into English by one of Carl Jung's students, Cary Baynes, and published in 1950 as *I Ching, The Book of Changes*. That same year Annie Hochberg-van Wallinga translated the German text of Wilhelm's book into Dutch, and Bruno Veneziani and A. G. Ferrara translated it into Italian. Translations in other European languages followed in fairly rapid succession.[35]

In certain respects Wilhelm's translation was like Legge's. It was heavily annotated, produced with assistance from a Chinese scholar (Lao Naixuan, 1843–1921), and based on the Qing dynasty's *Balanced Compendium on the Zhou Changes*, which gave the document a decidedly Neo-Confucian cast. But Wilhelm's translation was far smoother, and it reflected a much different worldview. The standard comparison of the two works—somewhat of a distortion on both ends—is that Legge's text indicates what the *Yijing* says while Wilhelm's conveys what it means.[36] In fact Wilhelm's rather didactic tone and his elaborate explanations of the features and functions of the *Changes* are strikingly reminiscent of primers such as the famous Ming dynasty work by Huang Chunyao (1605–45) titled *Understanding the Yijing at a Glance*.[37]

Another interesting point about Wilhelm's translation is that it bespeaks a person who not only was in love with China but also believed that the *Yijing* had something important to say to all humankind. Like Bouvet he considered the *Changes* to be a global property and a work of timeless wisdom. Unlike Bouvet, however, he treated it solely as a Chinese document, with no genetic links with either the ancient West or the Near East. This said, it should be noted that Wilhelm—like many scholars before him in both Asia and Europe—tried to domesticate the *Yijing* in various ways. One was to call on the authority of classical German philosophers and literary figures like Kant and Goethe to illustrate "parallel" ideas expressed in the *Changes*. Another was to cite the Bible for the same purpose. Yet another was to argue that the *Yijing* reflected "some common foundations of humankind," which all cultures were based on, albeit "unconsciously and unrecognizedly." Wilhelm believed, in other words, that "East and West belong inseparably together and join hands in mutual completion." The West, he argued, had something to learn from China.[38]

Wilhelm also tried to "demystify" the *Changes* by providing elaborate commentaries that paraphrased and explained away the "spiritual" material that he felt might "confuse the European reader too much with the unusual." This strategy of "rationalization" was somewhat similar to that of the Jesuit Figurists, "who frequently prepared second translations of certain texts because they claimed to know the intrinsic meaning of these texts: the prefiguration of Christian revelation."[39] In the case of the Figurists, this process often involved the willful misrepresentation (or at least the ignoring) of traditional commentaries in order to "dehistoricize" the "original" text. But in Wilhelm's case, most of his interpretations reflected the basic thrust of Cheng-Zhu orthodoxy as reflected in the *Balanced Compendium on the Zhou Changes*. Moreover they fit the general climate of rational academic discourse in early-twentieth-century Europe. Wilhelm remained a missionary, so to speak, but a secular one whose rendering of the *Changes* seemed to confirm Carl Jung's theories about archetypes and "synchronicity"—just as Bouvet's representations of the work had confirmed Leibniz's binary system and fed his speculations about a "Universal Characteristic."

By contrast, Aleister Crowley (1875–1947), an enthusiastic British exponent of Theosophy who traveled to China during the first decade of the twentieth century, adopted a self-consciously mystical approach to the *Changes*—a harbinger of countercultural enthusiasm for the document that would peak worldwide in the 1960s and 1970s. Upon his return from China, Crowley undertook the study of various Chinese texts, including the *Yijing*. He relied heavily at first on Legge's translation but found it wanting—not least because of the Scottish missionary-translator's hostility to the document ("what pitiable pedantic imbecility," Crowley once wrote of Legge's attitude). Eventually he developed an approach to the classic that dispensed with the conventional attributes of some of the trigrams and tried to assimilate them, in the fashion of Bouvet, into the kabbalistic "Tree of Life."

According to Crowley the *Yijing* "is mathematical and philosophical in form," and its structure "is cognate with that of the *Qabalah* [*Kabbala*]." The identity is so intimate, he claims, that "the existence of two such superficially different systems is transcendent testimony to the truth of both." In Crowley's view the *Dao* as expressed in the *Yijing* was "exactly equivalent to the Ain or Nothingness of our *Qabalah*," and the notions of yang and yin "correspond exactly with Lingam and Yoni." Furthermore he equated the Chinese idea of "essence" with Nephesh ("anima soul"), "qi" with Ruach ("intellect"), and "soul" with Neschamah (the "intuitive mind"). For Crowley the Confucian virtues of benevolence, moral duty, ritual propriety, and humane wisdom suggested the kabbalistic principles of "Geburah, Chesed, Tiphareth, and Daath."[40]

In Crowley's decidedly sexual interpretation of the *Changes*, reminiscent of McClatchie's, the eight trigrams represent (1) the male and female reproductive organs, (2) the sun and the moon, and (3) the four Greek elements—earth, air, fire, and water. The table on page 193 gives the highly imaginative Kabbalistic correlations identified by Crowley.

With similar abandon Crowley equates the four attributes of the judgment for the first hexagram, Qian— *yuan*, *heng*, *li*, and *zhen*—with the four spheres of the Tree of Life and the four parts of the human soul, representing wisdom, intuition, reason, and the animal soul.[41]

In more recent times a great many books and articles have attempted to relate the *Yijing* to the values of Christianity and/or Judaism and to employ Figurist techniques and logic. Representative works include Joe E. McCaffree's massive *Bible and I Ching Relationships* (1982; first published in 1967); C. H. Kang and Ethel R. Nelson's *The Discovery of Genesis* (1979); Hean-Tatt Ong's *The Chinese Pakua* (1991); and Jung Young Lee's *Embracing Change: Postmodern Interpretations of the I Ching from a Christian Perspective*

Kabbala Symbolism		*Changes* Symbolism	
Sefirah	Meaning	Trigram	Meaning
Daath	Supernatural Triad Knowledge	Qian	Heaven
Malkuth	Kingdom, Physical World	Kun	Earth
Chesed	Water, Mercy	Dui	Lake
Geburah	Fire, Strength	Zhen	Quake, Thunder
Netzach	Earth, Victory	Gen	Restraint, Mountain
Sephira Hod	Airy, Splendid	Sun	Compliance, Wind
Tiphareth	Spirituality, Beauty	Li	Cohesion, Fire
Yesod	Moon, Foundation	Kan	Sinkhole, Water

(1994). In addition to religiously oriented texts of this sort, many New Age or special interest versions of the *Changes* have appeared during the past few decades, bearing titles such as *The I Ching and Transpersonal Psychology, Self-Development with the I Ching, The I Ching Of Goddess, I Ching Divination for Today's Woman, The I Ching Tarot, Death and the I Ching, The I Ching on Love, Karma and Destiny, The I Ching of Management: An Age-Old Study for New Age Managers*, and my personal favorite, *The Golf Ching: Golf Guidance and Wisdom from the I Ching.* Many of these works are not actually translations, and some of them are quite amusing. Cassandra Eason, author of *I Ching Divination for Today's Woman*, for instance, writes: "While our mighty hunters are keeping a weather eye for potential concubines on the 17.22 from Waterloo to Woking, the Woman's *I Ching* uses the back door to enlightenment."[42]

Dozens of more rigorous translations of the *Changes* have appeared in print since the 1960s, in a variety of Western languages.[43] As with earlier academic renderings of the *Yijing*, they all have value and they all have limitations—in part because, as Daniel Gardner reminds us, "there simply is no one stable or definitive reading of a canonical text."[44]

The *Yijing* in Modern Western Culture: A Few Case Studies

From the 1960s onward, the influence of the *Changes* has been substantial and persistent in the West, but less as a cultural phenomenon than as a countercultural one. Putting scholarly interest aside, its appeal can be explained primarily by the challenge the book seems to pose to conventional Western values. Ironically, however, it has been heavily commercialized in recent years, as can be seen from the volume by Edward Hacker, Steve Moore, and Lorraine Patsco titled *I Ching: An Annotated Bibliography* (2002). This work evaluates more than a thousand *Changes*-related products designed for English-language speakers alone—mostly books, dissertations, articles, and reviews, but also records, tapes, CDs, videos, computer software, cards, kits, and other devices. The number of these products has increased steadily, and sometimes dramatically, in recent years, and they have reached virtually all parts of the Western world as well as Asia.[45]

As a child of the 1960s and 1970s, I still recall vividly the many ways that the *Yijing* entered the counterculture of the United States. One of them was through an enormously influential book by Fritjof Capra titled *The Tao of Physics: An Exploration of the Parallels between Modern Physics and Eastern Mysticism* (1975). As the subtitle suggests, Capra's basic idea was that an affinity exists between the ideas of quantum mechanics and various Eastern philosophies. In his view the *Yijing* provided an excellent example of quantum field theory—S-matrix theory in particular—and of "the dynamic aspect of all phenomena."[46] By the time *The Tao of Physics* appeared in print, Asia had begun to figure prominently in the media in the United States (thanks in particular to China's Cultural Revolution and the Vietnam War), and government support for Asian studies had begun to influence the curriculum of American colleges and universities nationwide.

Capra's book, which would soon become a best seller, received a highly favorable review in *Physics Today* (August 1976) from Victor Mansfield, a professor of physics and astronomy at Colgate University, who had himself written various papers and books connecting physics to both Buddhism and Jungian psychology. Other reviewers, however, were far less charitable—especially since the November Revolution of 1974, which marked the discovery of the so-called Psi particle, had fundamentally undermined the version of quantum mechanics that Capra happened to be expounding. But Capra's critics missed the point in a certain sense: he was not writing physics; he was writing "modern mystical literature."[47] And this literature was powerfully attractive, especially if it had the imprimatur of modern science.

An article that Capra wrote in 2002, titled "Where Have All the Flowers Gone? Reflections on the Spirit and Legacy of the Sixties," captures some of the attraction, although it fails to mention dramatic curricular changes in postsecondary education and the powerful countercultural forces exerted by the political and social movements of the time, which focused on the Vietnam War, civil rights, women's liberation, and more general issues of political and personal freedom (including sexual liberation). He writes: "The radical questioning of authority and the expansion of social and transpersonal consciousness [in the 1960s] gave rise to a whole new culture—a 'counterculture'—that defined itself in opposition to the dominant 'straight' culture by embracing a different set of values." The members of this alternative culture, who were called "hippies" by outsiders, possessed a strong sense of community. Capra notes: "Our subculture was immediately identifiable and tightly bound together. It had its own rituals, music, poetry, and literature; a common fascination with spirituality and the occult; and the shared vision of a peaceful and beautiful society. . . . In our homes we would frequently burn incense and keep little altars with eclectic collections of statues of Indian gods and goddesses, meditating Buddhas, yarrow stalks or coins for consulting the *I Ching*, and various personal 'sacred' objects."[48]

This account rings true as far as it goes. But two things are lost in it: First is the fact that one did not have to be a hippie to explore and experiment; "straights" discovered that they could also join the fun. Second is the fact that youthful exploration and experimentation went on in much of the rest of the world in the 1960s and 1970s, not just in the United States. The major centers of countercultural activity in the Western world were San Francisco, New York, London, Paris, Amsterdam, West Berlin, and Mexico City.

One of the most remarkable efforts to link the *Yijing* to the drug culture of the 1960s and 1970s was a book by Terence McKenna and Dennis McKenna titled *The Invisible Landscape: Mind, Hallucinogens, and the I Ching* (1975). In it the authors combine investigations into "the molecular basis of Amazonian shamanic trance" with speculations about the divinatory functions, calendrics, alchemy, and mathematics of the *Changes*. Their particular interest is in the way "different chemical waves" that are "characteristic of life" are reflected in the patterns of trigrams and hexagrams in the Yijing—Shao Yong's Later Heaven sequence of the hexagrams in particular.[49]

Aside from drugs, the most productive path to spiritual liberation in the Western counterculture appeared to be psychological. In 1961, after about a decade on the American scene as a rather cumbersome two-volume set, a handy one-volume edition of Richard Wilhelm's *The I Ching or Book of Changes*, with Carl Jung's original foreword, appeared in print. Jung's foreword, designed explicitly to illustrate the method of the *Changes* by means of a detailed divination, emphasized the need for honest reflection and acute self-awareness. "Even to the most biased eye," Jung states, "it is obvious that this book represents one long admonition to careful scrutiny of one's own character, attitude, and motives."[50]

The notion of creative self-understanding proved to be extremely appealing not only to laypersons but also to clinical practitioners, leading in time to a branch of Jungian psychology that increasingly used the *Yijing* as a therapeutic device. An early example can be found in Jolande Jacobi's essay in Jung's *Man and His Symbols* (1964), in which Jacobi's patient, "Henry," on his therapist's advice, uses the *Changes* to interpret a dream. Uncannily (or not), the symbolism of the two primary trigrams of the chosen hexagram, Meng (number 4, "Youthful Folly" in Wilhelm's rendering), coincided precisely with the symbols that had emerged in Henry's recent dreams, provoking a breakthrough in his therapy.[51]

In 1965 the self-styled Buddhist "missionary" John Blofeld published a short, inexpensive, and easy-to-read version of the classic titled *I Ching, the Book of Change*. This work—expressly designed "for those who wish to live in harmonious accord with nature's decrees but who naturally find them too inscrutable to be gathered from direct experience"—contributed substantially to public interest in the document.[52]

Soon references to the *Changes* began to appear everywhere in Western popular culture. As early as November 27, 1965, Bob Dylan gave an interview published in the *Chicago Daily News* in which he described the *Yijing* as "the only thing that is amazingly true, period." He added: "besides being a great book to believe in, it's also very fantastic poetry."[53] In 1966 Allen Ginsberg, founding father of the Beat generation of the 1950s and a major countercultural figure of the 1960s, wrote a widely distributed poem titled "Consulting *I Ching* Smoking Pot Listening to the Fugs Sing Blake." John Lennon sang of the *Changes* in "God" (1970), and the *New York Sessions* version of Dylan's acclaimed "Idiot Wind," recorded in the mid-1970s, contains the following line: "I threw the *I-Ching* yesterday, it said there might be some thunder at the well."[54] (Either Dylan has his trigrams and hexagrams mixed up here or he has produced a very sophisticated reading of the relationship between the Zhen hexagram, number 51, and the Jing hexagram, number 48.)

Perhaps the most famous example of an early *Yijing*-inspired literary work in the West is Philip K. Dick's award-winning novel *The Man in the High Castle* (1962). It tells the story of America in the early sixties, some twenty years after defeat by Nazi Germany and Japan in a titanic war has resulted in joint military occupation of the United States. Slavery is legal, anti-Semitism is rampant, and "the *I Ching* is as common as the Yellow Pages." Dick used the Wilhelm version of the *Changes* on several occasions in devising the plot (which has no denouement because, he later claimed, the *Yijing* provided no clear guidance), and he also integrated the work directly into the text. Nearly every character in the book consults the hexagrams, which naturally foreshadow the events that will unfold.[55] Like the poetry of Ginsberg and the lyrics of Dylan and others, Dick's novel both reflected the cultural importance of the *Changes* at the time and contributed substantially to it.

In Europe the influential French novelist and poet Raymond Queneau (1903–76) had a long-standing and intense interest in the *Yijing* (initially sparked by Philastre's translation and later reignited by Wilhelm's).[56] From 1960 to the early 1970s, he largely abandoned numerology and occult metaphysics in favor of a more "modern" view of mathematical structures and properties, but he returned to numerology in his last major work, a collection of prose poems titled *Morale élementaire* (Elementary Morality; 1975). The theme of these verses is one of constant mutation—in Queneau's words, the idea that what has changed has "really changed and it will change again."[57]

Here is an example of one piece that cleverly inter-mingles yin and yang imagery from the *Changes*:

> Everything started up the moment the sun rose. The mare pulls the cart, the bullock slips on its yoke, the rooster again sings its parting song. On the white leaf there is just one mark while the green one multiplies into myriad images. On hearing all this the rock no longer waits for either the crowd or the chisel. It is the beginning of the recording of all things. The ge-ometer considers the empty ensemble and deduces from it the sequence of whole numbers. Irrationals and transcendants step in to nourish their uncount-able thread. The grammarian discovers the passive conjugation. The child—it is a girl—sculpts a fairy from unctuous wax, plastic and polychromatic.[58]

This short prose poem is based ostensibly on the at-tributes of the Kun hexagram (number 2, "Receptive" in the Wilhelm translation), which are generally viewed as yin qualities: earth, passivity, femininity, and so forth. The judgment of the hexagram emphasizes the value of perseverance in the mare, and in keeping with the yin theme, we find not only an expressly fe-male horse at the beginning of the work but also an expressly feminine child at the end of it—not to men-tion an expressly feminine "model/subject." There is also emptiness and parting. Even the grammatical voice is passive. In Queneau's synoptic plan of the third section of *Morale élémentaire*, he refers to "passivity, the birth of all things."

Yet most of the remaining symbolism in the piece is decidedly yang. The mare, bull, and rooster act assertively; the stone is no longer passive; the child actively fashions something; and there are several beginnings (yang): the start of a day, with sunrise and a cock crowing; multiplicity from oneness; and something from nothing.[59] Thus in a single poem Queneau has not only encapsulated a dynamic yet traditional Chinese worldview based on the theme of yin-yang alternation, interaction, and interpenetration, but also a modern Western one, based on the language of numbers.

If we turn our gaze to Latin America, we see further evidence of the global spread of the *Changes*, exemplified by Jorge Luis Borges's famous poem "Para una Versión del *I King*" (For a Version of the *Yijing*). Jose Luis Ibañez of the Universidad Nacional Autunoma de Mexico tells us: "I learned to consult it [the *Yijing*] when Octavio Paz taught me in 1958. Back then we could only read Wilhelm's version in English with that amazing introduction by Carl Jung. A few years later the Beatles, with their attention on the Orient, contributed to the popularization of the document as one that was . . . [within] the reach of everyone."[60]

Of the many Mexican writers influenced by the *Changes*—including Salvador Elizondo, José Agustín, Jesús Gonzalez Dávila, Juan Tovar, Francisco Cervantes, Sergio Fernández, Daniel Sada, Alberto Blanco, Francisco Serrano, and José López Guido—Octavio Paz, a 1990 Nobel Prize winner in Literature, is perhaps the best known. Long enamored of Asia, he traveled there as early as 1951 and obtained an English-language version of Wilhelm's translation of the *Yijing*, which remained among his most beloved books until the day he died in 1998.

During the late 1960s and early 1970s, Paz, like Queneau, developed an international network of writers, artists, and musicians, many of whom drew upon the *Yijing* for creative inspiration. Locally, one of the most distinguished of these individuals was José Agustín. Agustín first encountered the *Changes* in the early sixties and instantly took to the book, fascinated by the notion that an image could be as expressive and powerful as a narrative, and by the idea that the *Yijing* could be used as a structuring device. His 1968 novel *Cerca del Fuego* (Near the Fire) is based on sixty-four separate texts, and many of its passages reflect descriptions of the hexagrams. In 1977 Agustín wrote an experimental work titled *El Rey se Acerca a Su Templo* (The King Approaches His Temple), which combines poetry and prose and also relies heavily on the *Yijing*. The first section, for instance, features the Lü hexagram ("Treading," number 10), and each of its six subheadings reflects its six lines.[61]

Another of Paz's close associates in Mexico was his disciple Francisco Serrano, who also experimented with the use of the *Changes* as a literary device, especially in poetic composition.[62] Among the visual artists in their creative circle were painters such as Arnaldo Coen, Arturo Rivera, Augusto Ramírez, and Felipe Erenberg, all of whom found inspiration and guidance in the *Yijing*. The same was true of the leading musician in the group, the composer Mario Lavista. Dramatists interested in the *Changes* included Hugo Argüelles, Emilio Carballido, and a younger generation represented by Carlos Olmos and González Dávila.

By virtue of their common interest in the *Changes*, several of these individuals, including Paz, Serrano, Coen, and Lavista, came to know the American composer John Cage, whose visit to Mexico City in 1976 to celebrate his sixty-fourth birthday provided the occasion for a creative collaboration involving design, music, and poetry titled *Mutaciones, Jaula, In/cubaciones* (Change, Cage, In/cubations). It may have been on this occasion that Paz used the *Yijing* to write a poem for Cage, who had become his good friend. After casting three coins and deriving a hexagram, Paz picked up a copy of Cage's book, *Silence*, and, guided by the *Changes* imagery he encountered, chose a few phrases from Cage's work to which he added some lines of his own.[63]

Cage deserved all this attention because he was, until his death in 1992, the foremost practitioner of *Yijing*-related music composition in the United States, with a global reputation and a worldwide network of followers. He first learned about the *Yijing* in 1936, and in the 1940s he occasionally consulted the Legge translation. But it was not until 1950—the year that Wilhelm's translation of the *Changes* first appeared in English—that he began composing with it, a practice he continued until the end of his career.

In 1951 Cage produced *Music of Changes*, one of his first fully "indeterminate" musical pieces, which identified the *Yijing* expressly as the source of his inspiration. A decade later, in his groundbreaking book of essays titled *Silence* (1961), which the critic John Rockwell of the *New York Times* described as "the most influential conduit of Oriental thought and artistic ideas into the artistic vanguard—not just in music but in dance, art and poetry as well,"[64] Cage describes how he created the two-part composition known as *Piano 21–56* (1955). Part of the process involved random operations with the *Yijing* to determine "the number of sounds per page." After establishing the clefs, bass or treble, with coin tosses, he then divided the sixty-four hexagram possibilities of the *Changes* into three categories: "normal (played on the keyboard); muted; and plucked (the two latter played on the strings of the piano)." For example, he writes, "a number 1 through 5 will produce a normal; 6 through 43 a muted; [and] 44 through 64 a plucked piano tone." Cage used a similar technique to determine whether a tone was natural, sharp, or flat, "the procedure being altered, of course, for the two extreme keys where only two possibilities exist."[65]

Cage did not use the *Yijing* simply to generate random numbers; he also cited its wisdom in essays and poetry, "asked it questions" in the course of composing, and relied on it for supplying rhythm and timing in much of his work. In *The Marrying Maiden: A Play of Changes* (1960), he and playwright Jackson Mac

Low used the hexagrams of the *Yijing* not only to produce the musical score but also to develop character and dialogue.[66] In addition Cage employed the *Changes* in the production of his striking visual art (he produced drawings, watercolors, and etchings, excellent examples of which can be seen in the 116 images in Kathan Brown's *John Cage—Visual Art: To Sober and Quiet the Mind*; 2000).

Cage's approach to the *Changes*, as he once described it, was to "ask the *I Ching* a question as though it were a book of wisdom, which it is." "What do you have to say about this?" he would ask, and then he would "just listen to what it says and see if some bells ring or not." On another occasion he remarked that he used the *Changes* "as a discipline, in order to free my work from my memory and my likes and dislikes." In 1988, toward the end of his life, he wrote: "I use the *I Ching* whenever I am engaged in an activity which is free of goal-seeking, pleasure giving, or discriminating between good and evil. That is to say, when writing poetry or music, or when making graphic works." He also used the *I Ching* as a book of wisdom, but not, he claimed, "as often as formerly."[67]

Cage's experimental music of the 1950s had broad repercussions. It is often credited with launching the Fluxus ("flowing") international network of artists, composers, and designers who were located in Europe (especially Germany) and Asia (especially Japan) as well as the United States—individuals who sought to blend different visual and musical media in creative ways.

Several composers found inspiration in Cage's work with the *Yijing*. One of the first of these was Udo Kasemets, an Estonian-born Canadian composer, conductor, pianist, organist, and writer. Like Cage, Kasemets used the *Changes* in his compositions and sometimes acknowledged it explicitly in the titles of his compositions—for instance, *Portrait: Music of the Twelve Moons of the I Ching: The Sixth Moon* (for piano, 1969); *I Ching Jitterbug: 50 Hz Octet* (8 winds/bowed strings, 1984); and *The Eight Houses of the I Ching* (for string quartet, 1990). The titles of Kasemets's compositions often reflect the human sources of his inspiration, which include many of the individuals discussed above: Cage (many times), Duchamp, Paz, and Cunningham (notably, the *John Cage/Octavio Paz Conjunction*, 1996). In 1984 Kasemets produced *4-D I Ching*, offering sixteen tapes with 4,096 combinations (the latter number represents the total possible permutations of the hexagram lines of the *Changes*: 64 × 64).

James Tenney is yet another famous composer inspired by Cage and the *Yijing*. Each of his *Sixty-Four Studies for Six Harps* (1985) is correlated with a hexagram, partly, as he put the matter, "for poetic/philosophical reasons, but also—perhaps more importantly—as a means of ensuring that all possible combinations of parametic states would be included in the work as a whole."[68] In Tenney's highly sophisticated and heavily mathematical work, each individual "study" is named after one of the sixty-four hexagrams. The correlations are based on configurations of adjacent digrams (two-lined structures; see chapter 3), each of which represents one of four possible states in a parameter: a broken (yin) line over a solid line (yang) is a low state; two broken lines is a medium state; a solid line over a broken line is a high state; and two solid lines is a full state. Thus hexagram 59 (Huan, or "Dispersion" in the Wilhelm translation used by Tenney), associated with Tenney's fifth study, has a high "pitch state," a medium "temporal density state," and a full "dynamic state." And then things get complicated.[69]

Among the many famous artists touched by John Cage's creativity was the dancer and choreographer Mercier ("Merce") Cunningham, who became Cage's life partner and frequent collaborator (they first met in the 1930s). One characteristic feature of Cunningham's performances is that he often used the *Yijing* to determine the sequence of his dances. Like Cage, Cunningham regularly collaborated with artists of other disciplines, including musicians such as David Tudor; visual artists such as Jasper Johns, Marcel Duchamp, Robert Rauschenberg, and Bruce Nauman; the designer Romeo Gigli; and the architect Benedetta Tagliabue.

Transnational collaboration and cross-fertilization of this sort profoundly influenced the intertwined worlds of avant-garde literature, music, and art in the 1960s, 1970s, and 1980s—and much more could certainly be said about the process. A great deal more might also be said about the way that organizations such as the Esalen Institute in Big Sur, California, and its various European counterparts served as venues for extensive and intensive cross-cultural and interdisciplinary conversations about language, art, literature, philosophy, religion, and science, many of which naturally involved the *Yijing*. Yet another fertile field of inquiry would be the worldwide explosion of interest in the theories and practices of fengshui and Traditional Chinese Medicine, both of which have long been closely linked to the philosophy and symbolism of the *Changes*.[70]

Still another fruitful approach to the spread of the *Yijing* in the West would be a systematic examination of the many books and articles on the mathematical and scientific applications of the *Changes* that have appeared over the past few decades. I have perused dozens of such works, with titles such as *Bagua Math*, *I-Ching Philosophy and Physics*, and *DNA and the Yijing*, both in print and in manuscript form. These studies are, to say the least, of remarkably uneven quality, but they are invariably fascinating.

Many such manuscripts have been deposited in the archives of the Needham Institute at Cambridge University, together with correspondence between the authors of these works and various luminaries, including Joseph Needham, Arnold Toynbee, and Francis H. C. Crick (codiscoverer of the double-helix structure of DNA in 1953, which won him the Nobel Prize in 1962). When Professor Needham received a copy of a work that seemed somehow to be beyond his vast competence, he would send it to a colleague, as he did with a 1973 manuscript titled "The *I-Ching*, The Unraveled Clock: Reconstruction of the Mathematical Science of Prehistoric China," written by a scholar self-described as a Harvard graduate and a former Ph.D. candidate at the University of Toronto in both anthropology and Chinese. Here is the letter that Professor Crick's secretary sent to the author of the manuscript on June 1, 1973:

> Dear _____ [I have elided the name for obvious reasons],
>
> Dr. Crick has asked me to return to you your manuscript entitled, "The *I-Ching*, The Unraveled Clock" as it appears to him to be complete nonsense from beginning to end.
>
> Yours sincerely,
>
> (Miss) Sue Barnes
> Secretary to
> Dr. F.H.C. Crick

Undaunted, this particular person went on to publish in the next two decades at least three books on the relationships among the *Yijing*, astronomy, mathematics, and chemistry.

Concluding Remarks

Despite the great and often glaring differences separating the *Yijing* from such religious classics as the Bible, the Talmud, the Qur'an, the Bhagavad Gita, and the Lotus Sutra, it deserves to be considered one of the great works of spiritually inspired world literature. Why? In the first place, the life cycle of the *Changes* has been surprisingly similar to that of the above-mentioned spiritually inspired books. In each case, for example, written commentaries have amplified, clarified, explained, and modified the meanings of the core text, ironing out inconsistencies and opening up new interpretive possibilities—including, of course, correlative and numerical ones.[1] In the process the commentaries have helped to establish these texts as foundational. Moreover, like other classic works, the *Changes* has enjoyed remarkable longevity—and it is still going strong. It has traveled widely and left enduring versions of itself in many parts of the world. At the same time, however, the reasons for its long life and global appeal have far more to do with its challenging content and multifarious applications than with any sort of religious attraction; the book certainly offers no prospect of other-worldly salvation, for instance.

The sustained appeal of the *Yijing* rests primarily in three related areas, all of which apply to many other classic works as well: (1) the intellectual challenges it poses, (2) the psychological insights it encourages, and (3) the creative inspiration it affords, not least by virtue of its powerful and pervasive symbolism. Having said a good deal about the first two points in previous chapters, let me conclude with a few brief remarks about the last point. These concluding remarks summarize and in some cases expand on a substantial amount of work that I have done previously on the cultural significance of the *Changes*.[2]

The symbolism of the *Yijing* appeared everywhere in premodern China, from written inscriptions and craft productions to art and architecture, and it continues to be manifest in certain realms of Chinese culture to this day. Remnants of its symbolism can also be found throughout most of the rest of contemporary East Asia, including Korea, Japan, Vietnam, and Tibet. Moreover at least some *Changes*-related symbols—notably the Diagram of the Supreme Ultimate, popularly known as the "yin-yang symbol" (figure 6.1)—have become decorative elements throughout much of the Western world, appearing, for example, on innumerable commercial products, from surfboards to jewelry.

The word magic of the *Yijing* has also been pervasive. During the entire imperial era in China and in Japan, Korea, and Vietnam for the past several centu-

FIGURE 6.1
The Supreme Ultimate Symbol

ries as well, a great many people, places, writings, art-
works, and buildings have borne names based on hexagrams or on characters selected from the basic text or
the Ten Wings of the *Changes*. Allusions to it could be
found everywhere. At the highest level of Chinese society, reign names often reflected concepts such as the
Supreme Ultimate or employed one or two of the four
characters that constitute the judgment of the Qian
hexagram (number 1): "Fundamentality," "Prevalence,"
"Fitness," and "Constancy" (also translated "Great,"
"Penetrating," "Proper," and "Right" or "Immoveable").
In the Forbidden City numerous expressions drawn
from the *Changes* appear either as inscriptions inside
the palace buildings or as the names of the buildings
themselves. At the lower levels of Chinese society, the
Yijing's magical language was also ubiquitous. Quite
apart from its use in fortune-telling, it could be found
in a great many personal names, New Year's couplets

and other auspicious inscriptions, and even popular proverbs—for instance, "Good fortune arises when misfortune peaks," derived directly from the hexagrams Tai ("Peace," number 11) and Pi ("Obstruction," number 12).

The eight trigrams—particularly Qian and Kun— were powerful visual symbols in all sectors of traditional Chinese society (and East Asia more generally), evident, for example, in the decorations of the Forbidden City, the Temples of Heaven and Earth, city god temples, Buddhist and Daoist religious establishments, and the households of both elites and commoners. They also adorned flags and other paraphernalia, not only in China but also in Korea, Japan, Vietnam, and Tibet. In most cases the trigrams served not only as decorations but also as talismans (see figure 6.2). In addition they gave their name to various martial arts practices, notably the Eight Trigram Hands. Although associated primarily with orthodox culture, they might also be appropriated by rebellious groups, such as the notorious Eight Trigrams Society of the late Qing period.

Philosophically speaking, the *Changes* exerted more influence in China than any other Confucian classic. It was the foundation of Chinese metaphysics and the locus classicus for most philosophical discussions of time and space. Its emphasis on correlative thinking and intuitive understanding left an enduring imprint on China for at least two thousand years. In premodern times no Chinese thinker of any stripe could afford

FIGURE 6.2
Trigrams on a Ritual Bell in the Shanghai City God Temple

to ignore the *Yijing* entirely. Moreover as early as the Han dynasty we see the emergence of highly influential derivative works, such as Jiao Yanshou's (ca. 70–10 BCE) *Forest of Changes*, Yang Xiong's (53 BCE–18 CE) *Classic of Great Mystery*, and several important apocryphal writings, including *Opening up the Regularities of Qian*. This process of creative inspiration persisted for many centuries and continues to this day.

Virtually all the major fortune-telling traditions of China (and of other countries in East Asia as well), including astrology, numerology, meteorological divination, geomancy, physiognomy, and fate calculation,

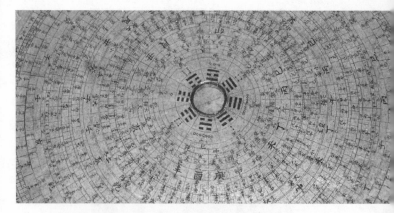

FIGURE 6.3
Detail of a Qing Dynasty Fengshui Compass
This imperially authorized compass, in the author's private
collection, measures 50.8 cm in diameter. It has a total of
forty-nine rings, all of which contain cosmological information
that had to be considered—at least theoretically—in fengshui
calculations. The cosmic variables in these rings include all those
discussed in this book and a great many more.

trace their origins to the *Yijing* and employ its diverse
symbolism. A fengshui compass, whether from China,
Japan, Korea, or Vietnam, provides a perfect working
model of the many cosmological variables that entered
into *Yijing* and other divinatory calculations (see figure 6.3).[3]

Some Chinese maps also indicate such variables.
Figure 6.4 shows the left section of a map titled "Fixed
Positions of Heaven and Earth," which illustrates the
cosmic power exerted by the eight trigrams and the
twenty-eight lunar lodges.

地方如棋局

地不滿東南

FIGURE 6.4

Qing Dynasty Map of the Fixed Positions of Heaven and Earth

This illustration, excerpted from a Qing dynasty almanac (1721), represents slightly more than half of a complete map showing the entire universe. Heaven, we are told, is round, encompassing the Earth "like an umbrella." The Earth is square, "like a chessboard." In the excerpt shown, five of the eight trigrams are depicted outside the celestial circle, along with most of the twenty-eight lunar lodges. The square territory influenced by these cosmological "force fields" includes virtually all of China proper, as well as Southeast Asia, Tibet, Central Asia, and lands far to the west described generically as the realm of the "Hundred Barbarians." From the British Library Board, the Oriental and India Office Collections of the British Library (#15257 a 24).

The symbols of the *Changes* were widely used in the description and evaluation of East Asian culture, from music, flower arranging, and cooking to literature, art, and architecture. Virtually any subject that had an aesthetic or metaphysical dimension came to be closely linked with the *Yijing*. Consider, for example, the opinions of Liu Xie (ca. 465–ca. 521 CE), a profoundly influential literary critic throughout the imperial era, who tells us in his *Literary Mind and the Carving of Dragons* that "the images of the *Yijing* first brought to light the spiritual presences that previously had been concealed," thus illuminating "human patterns." Throughout this work Liu repeatedly and reverentially cites the *Changes*—not only as the foundation of Chinese aesthetics, but also as a concrete model for various literary forms and genres.[4]

The *Yijing* informed Chinese artistic and literary criticism in other ways as well. The hexagram Bi (number 22), for example, came to denote beauty, grace, and simplicity of form, while Yu (number 16) suggested energy, enthusiasm, and emotion. Kuai (number 43) stood for resolute, critical judgment; Li (number 30), for logical clarity. Qian (number 1) generally referred to creativity and spirituality, while Kun (number 2) indicated passive intelligence. Hexagrams also became a tool of literary analysis. For example Zhang Xinzhi's late-Qing interpretation of the great eighteenth-century novel *Dream of the Red Chamber* uses hexagram relationships to analyze the personalities of certain important characters.

The *Yijing* provided a cosmologically grounded justification for the social and political hierarchies of imperial China from the Han period through the Qing. As one of many indications, the extraordinarily influential Neo-Confucian compilation known as the *Jinsi lu* (Reflections on Things at Hand) employs about fifty different hexagrams to illustrate various social and political roles and relationships. Hexagrams also played a part in the administration of law, as we have already seen in the case of the Kangxi emperor's contemplation of the Shihe hexagram (chapter 3). Other law-related hexagrams include Kan ("Sinkhole," number 29), Zhongfu ("Inner Trust," number 61), Xie ("Release," number 40), Song ("Contention," number 6), Lü ("The Wanderer," number 56), and Feng ("Abundance," number 55).

One of the most pervasive uses of *Yijing* symbolism in premodern China was in the related realms of science and medicine. As we have seen, until the dawn of the twentieth century, most Chinese intellectuals believed that the *Changes* had the capacity to explain virtually everything in nature.[5] The official eighteenth-century assessment of the classic by the editors of the *Complete Collection of the Four Treasuries* was that "the way of the *Changes* is broad and great. It encompasses everything, [providing the foundation for] astronomy, geography, music, military methods, the study of rhymes, numerical calculations, and alchemy."[6] Even individuals such as Fang Yizhi and Jiang Yong, who possessed a substantial knowledge of Western science and had a deep interest in the role of numbers in explaining natural relationships and processes, believed that the eternal principles of astronomy, calendrics, mathematics, music, and medicine could all be found in the Yellow River Chart, the Luo River Writing, hexagrams, trigrams, and their individual lines.

The index to almost any volume of Joseph Needham's monumental *Science and Civilisation in China* (more than two dozen at the time of this writing) under the subject heading "*I Ching*" will reveal that there were very few realms in the natural world for which the *Changes* did not provide some sort of meaningful explanation. The color and flow of blood, the anatomy of crustaceans, the physical constitution of people from different areas of China, the movements of the eye and jaw, acupuncture and pulse points, chemical and alchemical reactions, the nature of earthquakes, musical tonality, and even male and female sexual responses could all be explained by reference to trigrams, hexagrams, or both.[7] Similarly Li Yang's *Book of Changes and Traditional Chinese Medicine*, an English-language distillation of his award-winning studies in Chinese, provides numerous examples of the way the eight trigrams and the number systems of the Yellow River Chart and the Luo River Writing, as well as yin-yang/five agents correlations, figure into Chinese traditions of healing, which remain vital to this day.[8]

This is not to say that empirical investigations were unimportant to premodern Chinese scientists and technicians. Needham's *Science and Civilisation in China* abundantly documents the ways that physicians experimented with herbal and other medicines, mathematicians solved complicated algebraic problems, astronomers carefully observed the heavens, geographers closely examined the earth, and all kinds of scientifically minded individuals investigated the realms of what would now be called physics, engineering, biology, and zoology.

But if Chinese intellectuals "were fully satisfied with an explanation they could find from the system of the *Book of Changes,* they would not go further to look for mathematical formulations and experimental verifications in their scientific studies."[9] The either/or question that might be posed by a scientist or physician relying primarily on deductive reasoning did not generally concern a Chinese theoretician, who naturally thought in terms of systematic correspondence. Thus in premodern China a way could usually be found "to reconcile opposing views and to build bridges—fragile as they may appear to the outside observer—permitting thinkers and practitioners to employ liberally all the concepts available, as long as they were not regarded as destructive to society."[10]

The twentieth century in China brought an appreciation for Western science and mathematics that went well beyond the enthusiasm that at least a few Chinese scholars had for the ideas introduced by the Jesuits in the seventeenth and eighteenth centuries. As in the past, scientifically minded individuals tried to use the *Yijing* to explain the natural world, but their efforts were now predicated on modern Western understandings of these realms of knowledge. The same was true of newly introduced theories of the humanities and the social sciences. Thus we see the eventual rise to prominence of Chinese scholars such as Shen Heyong, whose pioneering studies have sought to show affinities between notions of "mind" as expressed in the hexagrams and Ten Wings of the *Changes* and in Jungian psychology.[11]

From the 1920s onward, Chinese scholars have relentlessly explored connections between the *Yijing* and newly introduced ideas from the West, from linear algebra and quantum mechanics to the fields of molecular biology and computer coding. Thus we have contemporary individuals such as Yang Li arguing in the same basic vein as Fang Yizhi and Jiang Yong in the Qing period that the numbers of the Yellow River Chart and the Luo River Writing are the "deriving coefficient" of everything in the cosmos.[12] Similarly Feng Youlan contends that the *Yijing* contains an incipient "algebra of the universe"; Xie Qiucheng maintains that the hexagrams of the classic were originally designed as a high-efficiency information-transfer system analogous to contemporary computer coding based on optimal units of two (the number of basic trigrams in each hexagram) and three (the number of lines in each trigram); and Tang Mingbang, drawing on the writings of Xie and other contemporary Chinese scholars, asserts that the forms of atomic structure in nuclear physics, the genetic code in molecular biology, and the eight-tier matrix in linear algebra all seem to be related to the logic of the *Changes*.[13] Although this sort of thinking remains essentially correlative, it has been nonetheless satisfying for Chinese scholars who have long been accustomed to the view that modern science had somehow passed China by.

What, then, does the future hold for the *Yijing*, both domestically and internationally? No one can answer this question with certainty, of course, but it will probably continue to serve as a source of inspiration for creative thinkers, East and West, as it has for many hundreds of years. It will also continue to be studied by Chinese scholars as a foundational cultural document, with possible practical applications in the modern world. And it will no doubt continue to be translated by foreigners eager to understand and transmit its arcane wisdom for scholarly purposes or commercial gain. Perhaps most important, it will continue to offer us new opportunities for the comparative study of the lives of great religious books—how they came to be born, how they evolved, and how they traveled across space and time. By engaging in such comparisons we will not only learn more about other cultures; we will also assuredly learn more about ourselves.

Notes

INTRODUCTION

1. Lynn, *Classic of Changes*, 62–65, modified.
2. See Hon, *The Yijing and Chinese Politics*, 3.
3. For different renderings of all sixty-four hexagram names, see http://chaocenter.rice.edu/Content. aspx?id=601.
4. Based on R. Wilhelm, *I Ching*, 200–201, but modified for clarity.
5. Ibid., 57–59; cf. Lynn, *Classic of Changes*, 216–21 and notes.

PART TWO   The Domestic Evolution of the *Yijing*

1. See the discussion in R. Smith, *Fathoming the Cosmos*, 241ff.
2. See R. Smith, *Fortune-tellers and Philosophers*, 120.

CHAPTER 1   Genesis of the *Changes*

1. Lynn, *Classic of Changes*, 77; cf. R. Wilhelm, *I Ching*, 328–29.
2. On Shang oracle bone divination, see Keightley, *Sources of Shang History*.

3. Shaughnessy, "Composition of the *Zhouyi*," 16–49. For arguments suggesting an earlier date, consult Cook, *Classical Chinese Combinatorics*, 417–39; and Marshall, *Mandate of Heaven*, 3–11, 35ff.

4. For a list of the sixty-four hexagrams in what became their conventional order, as well as various English translations of the hexagram names, see http://chao-center.rice.edu/Content.aspx?id=601.

5. See, for example, Shaughnessy, "Composition of the *Zhouyi*," 112–23. For some interesting speculations, inspired largely by traditional Chinese interpretations, see Wei, *Exposition*, 47–60.

6. As indicated in the introduction, Gen has been variously translated as Mountain, Restraint, Keeping Still, Bound, Stabilizing, Limited, Immobile, Steadiness, etc. The translations below follow Richard Kunst, "Original *Yijing*." Cf. Rutt, *Zhouyi*; and Gotshalk, *Divination, Order, and the Zhouyi*.

7. Kunst, "Original *Yijing*," 342–43. In this rendering, *gen* serves as a loan word for *ken*, "to open up," referring presumably to a sacrificial victim.

8. See Shaughnessy, "Composition of the *Zhouyi*," 121–22.

9. For extensive discussions of the variant understandings of these cryptic formulas, see Kunst, "Original *Yijing*," 150–211, 369–80, 421–38. Cf. Shaughnessy, "Composition of the *Zhouyi*," 123–35, 175–287.

10. The term that I have rendered as "successful" (*heng*) often carries the meaning of a similar-looking and similar-sounding word for "sacrificial offerings." Overall the most positive term ("auspicious") outnumbers the most negative term ("ominous") almost 3 to 1.

11. For detailed discussions of the linguistic and literary devices employed in the *Changes*, consult Kunst, "Original *Yijing*," 19–95; and Shaughnessy, "Composition of the *Zhouyi*," 104–68, 135–287.

12. An exception is Rutt's *Zhouyi*, which reflects rhymes and other structural features of the judgments and line statements. Kunst, "Original *Yijing*," indicates rhyme schemes by a system of subscript letters explained on page xvi.

13. Kunst, "Original *Yijing*," 345, modified.

14. Ibid., 301, modified. Cf. Shaughnessy, "Composition of the *Zhouyi*," 162–63, 183–85.

15. For an illuminating discussion of Bronze Age China, consult Rutt, *Zhouyi*, 5–25. Cf. Kunst, "Original *Yijing*," 10–16; and Gotshalk, *Divination, Order, and the Zhouyi*, 3–36.

16. See Shaughnessy, "Composition of the *Zhouyi*," 268–87; and the extended discussion in Kunst, "Original *Yijing*," 369–420. The rendering "gorged dragon" represents an effort to combine the idea of a gorge or "gully" with the term designating the "neck" of the dragon in the Canlong constellation.

17. The animal identified here as a dragon (*long*) should not be confused with the dragon of Western lore. By Han times at the latest, the imagery of dragons was overwhelmingly positive.

18. See the extended discussion in Shaughnessy, "Composition of the *Zhouyi*," 266–87. Cf. Kunst, "Original *Yijing*," 369–420.

19. See, for example, Marshall, *Mandate of Heaven*; and Shaughnessy, "Marriage, Divorce and Revolution."

20. K. Smith, "*Zhouyi* Divination," 447–50. Cf. Xing, "Hexagram Pictures," 598.

21. See K. Smith, "*Zhouyi* Divination," 430–31, modified.

22. Ibid. Cf. Rutt, *Zhouyi*, 179–80.

23. K. Smith, "*Zhouyi* Divination," 430–31.

24. According to the *Rites of Zhou*, a late Warring States work, there were two hexagram-based compilations that preceded the *Zhou Changes*. One of these, known as the *Linked Mountains* and identified with the Xia dynasty, reportedly began with the Gen hexagram (number 52 in the received version). The other, known as *Return to the Hidden* and identified with the Shang dynasty, reportedly began with the Kun hexagram (number 2 in the received order).

25. See the translation by Shaughnessy, *I Ching*; cf. D. Wang, *Les signes et les mutations*.

26. Shaughnessy, *I Ching*, 241–42, modified. For the idea that "to prognosticate without virtue" is inappropriate to the *Changes*, see ibid., 233.

27. Ibid., 241–42, modified significantly. See also ibid., 197, 219, where Confucius reportedly describes the *Changes* as an effective device for "penetrating numbers" and "taking numbers to their limit."

CHAPTER 2 The Making of a Classic

1. See Shaughnessy, *I Ching*, 17, 229, and 237.

2. A. Meyer et al., "Cosmic Resonance Theory," 3.

3. Nathan Sivin, cited in C. Cullen, "The Science/Technology Interface," 301.

4. A. Meyer et al., "Cosmic Resonance Theory."

5. Roth, "Psychology and Self-Cultivation," 645–46.

6. Cited in de Bary and Bloom, *Sources of Chinese Tradition*, 1:338.

7. A. Meyer et al., "Cosmic Resonance Theory."

8. Needham, *Science and Civilisation*, 2:280–81. Cf. Field, *Ancient Chinese Divination*, 7–20; and Hall and Ames, *Anticipating China*, esp. 123–41, 183–202, 237–68.

9. See A. Meyer et al., "Cosmic Resonance Theory." Cf. Hall and Ames, *Anticipating China*, 256ff., esp. 264–68.

10. See, for example, Lynn, *Classic of Changes*, 2–4; and R. Wilhelm, *I Ching*, lxi–lxii, 255–61.

11. For an excellent overview of the language and purposes of the document, see Peterson, "Making Connections."

12. Lynn, *Classic of Changes*, 51, 62, modified slightly; cf. R. Wilhelm, *I Ching*, 294, 314.

13. Lynn, *Classic of Changes*, 56–57; cf. R. Wilhelm, *I Ching*, 304.

14. See Ming Dong Gu, "Elucidation of Images," 471–73; also Wang and Zhang, "Roots"; Zhang, "*Book of Changes*"; and Zheng, "Process Thinking."

15. Lynn, *Classic of Changes*, 60–63, slightly modified; cf. R. Wilhelm, *I Ching*, 307–14.

16. Lynn, *Classic of Changes*, 67; cf. R. Wilhelm, *I Ching*, 322.

17. Lynn, *Classic of Changes*, 49–50; cf. R. Wilhelm, *I Ching*, 287–88.

18. Lynn, *Classic of Changes*, 50, modified; cf. R. Wilhelm, *I Ching*, 290.

19. Quoted in Lynn, *Classic of Changes*, 84; cf. R. Wilhelm, *I Ching*, 342. See also Lynn, *Classic of Changes*,

58, 63, 69n7, 85, 91, 99n35, 135, 141n6, 157n5, 237, 240n5, 263, 267–68, 362n8, 463, 498.

20. Lynn, *Classic of Changes*, 63; cf. R. Wilhelm, *I Ching*, 315.

21. Lynn, *Classic of Changes*, 120–21; cf. R. Wilhelm, *I Ching*, 265–67.

22. See Shaughnessy, *I Ching*, 54–55; and Lynn, *Classic of Changes*, 466–70.

23. This translation is based on Lynn, *Classic of Changes*, 466–70, with several modifications.

24. Variant characters in the Mawangdui version of this line suggest the idea of "scratching the spine" rather than "splitting the back flesh." See Shaughnessy, *I Ching*, 55, 292.

25. See, for example, the divergent opinions offered by Kong Yingda, Cheng Yi, and Zhu Xi cited in Lynn, *Classic of Changes*, 470–72, notes 3–8.

26. Lynn, *Classic of Changes*, 216, modified; cf. R. Wilhelm, *I Ching*, 452.

27. Lynn, *Classic of Changes*, 217; cf. R. Wilhelm, *I Ching*, 453.

28. Lynn, *Classic of Changes*, 120–21; cf. R. Wilhelm, *I Ching*, 265–67.

29. Lynn, *Classic of Changes*, 121–24; cf. R. Wilhelm, *I Ching*, 265–79.

30. Ibid (both sources).

31. Lynn, *Classic of Changes*, 80–81, 90–92; cf. R. Wilhelm, *I Ching*, 337–38, 349–51.

32. Lynn, *Classic of Changes*, 103; cf. R. Wilhelm, *I Ching*, 276.

33. See Lynn, *Classic of Changes*, 113–16, slightly modified; cf. R. Wilhelm, *I Ching*. Wilhelm divides this com-

mentary, which he translates as "Miscellaneous Notes," under each individual hexagram in Book III.

34. Lynn, *Classic of Changes*, 87–89, modified; cf. R. Wilhelm, *I Ching*, 345–48.

35. Lynn, *Classic of Changes*, 87; cf. R. Wilhelm, *I Ching*, 345.

36. Shaughnessy, *I Ching*, 151, 317–18.

CHAPTER 3 Interpreting the *Changes*

1. Wei, *Exposition*, provides an excellent English-language example of traditional approaches to *Yijing* scholarship and divination, focusing primarily on the Qian and Kun hexagrams.

2. For details, see B. Wang, "Study of Ancient and Modern Text Classics."

3. Lynn, *Classic of Changes*, 54, 62–63; cf. R. Wilhelm, *I Ching*, 300, 314–15.

4. Lynn, *Classic of Changes*, 60; cf. R. Wilhelm, *I Ching*, 308. See also Goodman, "Exegetes and Exegesis," 290–310.

5. Lynn, *Classic of Changes*, 60–62; cf. R. Wilhelm, *I Ching*, 310–13. For details, see Adler, *Introduction*, 33–47.

6. See Lynn, *Classic of Changes*, 72–73, notes 34–40, for a few illustrations. Granet, *La Pensée chinoise*, esp. 91–178 ("Les nombres"), provides an extended discussion of the power of numbers in traditional Chinese culture. See also Goodman, "Exegetes and Exegesis," 290–302; and Ding, "Numerical Mysticism."

7. B. Wang's "Study of Ancient and Modern Text Classics," 59, describes Jing's approach to the *Changes* as

"situated in the middle" of the New Text and Old Text traditions.

8. See Meyer, "Correct Meaning," 44–48.

9. For details on these and related systems, see Nielsen, *Companion*, 1–6 (Eight Palaces), 7–9 (Six Positions), 59–62 ("Flying and Hiding"), 67–69 (Stems and Branches), 75–89 (Hexagram Breaths), 180–84 (Inserted Stem and Inserted Musical Notes), 204–8 (Ascent and Descent), 274–76 (Waxing and Waning), etc. Some of these techniques have been attributed to other individuals. See also Goodman, "Exegetes and Exegesis," 168–74.

10. See Nielsen, *Companion*, 275–76.

11. See ibid., 45 (on matching positions) and 111–14 (on nuclear trigrams, described by Nielsen as "interlocking trigrams"). For a thorough discussion of the notion of "line positions," consult ibid., 294–99.

12. Lynn, *Classic of Changes*, 538; cf. R. Wilhelm, *I Ching*, 710.

13. Ibid. (both sources).

14. For details, see R. Wilhelm, *I Ching*, 360–65; also Nielsen, *Companion*, 294–99, 333.

15. Nielsen, *Companion*, 111–14.

16. R. Wilhelm, *I Ching*, 709–13, discusses the implications of the relative positions of the nuclear trigrams for an understanding of the Jiji hexagram. Cf. Lynn, *Classic of Changes*, 538–44.

17. For details on these individuals, see Goodman, "Exegetes and Exegesis," esp. 154–88, 240–310.

18. For some examples of Zheng's general interpretive approach, see Meyer, "Correct Meaning," 83–86, 104–14; also Goodman, "Exegetes and Exegesis," 183–85.

19. For brief discussions of this substantial apocryphal literature, see Nielsen's *Companion*, 304, 306–7.

20. See the discussion in R. Wilhelm, *I Ching*, 359–60.

21. See Nielsen, *Companion*, 294–300.

22. Ibid., 308.

23. See ibid., 20, 185–87, and 315–17. Wei, *Exposition*, 198–99, maintains that "in nine cases out of ten, the meaning of one line is confirmed and elucidated by the significance of its transformation."

24. Cited in Shaughnessy, "Commentary," 227, modified.

25. On Wang Bi's highly influential *Yijing* scholarship, see Tze-ki Hon, "Human Agency"; also Goodman, "Exegetes and Exegesis," 240–379; and Lynn, *Classic of Changes*, esp. 10–18, 25–39.

26. Lynn, *Classic of Changes*, 32, conveys Wang's disdain for Late Han interpretive techniques.

27. Ibid., 26, modified.

28. Hon, "Hexagrams and Politics," 15.

29. Lynn, *Classic of Changes*, 29, 466–72.

30. For the ideas and activities of other *Yijing* enthusiasts during the Six Dynasties period, see Goodman, "Exegetes and Exegesis."

31. Nielsen, *Qian zuo du*, 91; see also Nielsen, *Companion*, 256.

32. Pregadio, *Great Clarity*, 216 ff.

33. For details and illustrations, see R. Smith, *Fathoming the Cosmos*, 107–11.

34. Cited in ibid., 216.

35. Nielsen, *Companion*, 103–5, 107–10, 169–71, 254–56, and 264–68, offers useful speculations about the origins of the illustrations to be discussed below.

36. For evidence that versions of these documents may

have existed in Han times, see ibid., 103–5, 169–71, and 236–37.

37. Adler, *Introduction*, 3–14; see also Nielsen, *Companion*, 103–5.

38. Adler, *Introduction*, 3–14; see also Nielsen, *Companion*, 169–71.

39. Lynn, *Classic of Changes*, 120–121; cf. R. Wilhelm, *I Ching*, 265–67.

40. Lynn, *Classic of Changes*, 121–22; cf. R. Wilhelm, *I Ching*, 267–71.

41. See, for example, Nielsen, *Companion*, 103–5, 169–71, 236–37, 254–56.

42. See R. Smith, *Fortune-tellers and Philosophers*, 70–74, 89–91.

43. On Shao, see Birdwhistell, *Transition to Neo-Confucianism*, esp. 71–123; cf. Adler, *Introduction*, 21–30; and K. Smith et al., *Sung Dynasty*, 100–35.

44. For the text of the Great Commentary, which served as foundation for this idea, see Lynn, *Classic of Changes*, 65–66; cf. R. Wilhelm, *I Ching*, 318–19.

45. Birdwhistell, *Transition*, esp. 50–94, 235–45. Shao uses the term "image" to refer to all categories of things, so that by knowing any one thing, a person "can unerringly infer its relationship to every other thing." See K. Smith et al., *Sung Dynasty*, 108.

46. K. Smith et al., *Sung Dynasty*, 110.

47. Ibid., 105ff.

48. For details, see ibid., 136–68.

49. For details on Zhu's life and his ideas on the *Changes*, see ibid., 169–205; also Chan, *Chu Hsi and Neo-Confucianism*, esp. 292–311.

50. Cited in R. Smith, *Fortune-tellers and Philosophers*, 94–95, slightly modified.

51. Cited in ibid.

52. For some examples of the similarities and differences between the views of Cheng Yi and Zhu Xi, see K. Smith et al., *Sung Dynasty*, 136–205; see also the notes to many of the translated individual hexagram texts in Lynn, *Classic of Changes*.

53. For details on this system, see Nielsen, *Companion*, 1–6; and R. Wilhelm, *I Ching*, 725–27.

54. Lo, "Change beyond Syncretism," esp. 281. Cleary, *Buddhist I Ching*, offers a loose but useful translation of this important text.

55. Cleary, *Taoist I Ching*, offers a loose but useful translation of this important text.

56. See the discussion in Wei, *Exposition*, 108–10.

57. See MacGillivray, "New Interpretation."

58. A number of talented Western scholars, beginning with Edward Shaughnessy and Richard Kunst in the 1980s, have used this archaeologically based Chinese scholarship to excellent effect.

59. For an excellent overview of *Changes* divination by a Chinese scholar-practitioner, see Wei, *Exposition*, 97–113.

60. Another process, considered unorthodox but widely practiced, involved coin tossing and was known as the "Forest of Fire Pearls Method" or the "King Wen Approach." See Lynn, *Classic of Changes*, 21–22; cf. R. Wilhelm, *I Ching*, 723–24.

61. For a detailed description of this process, see Wei, *Exposition*, 100–107; cf. Lynn, *Classic of Changes*, 19–21; and R. Wilhelm, *I Ching*, 721–23.

62. For a discussion of the numerology involved, see Adler, *Introduction*, 33–47. Cf. Lynn, *Classic of Changes*, 60–62; and R. Wilhelm, *I Ching*, 308–13.

63. Adler, *Introduction*, 49–53, modified. Each type of hexagram is illustrated with historical examples provided by Cai Yuanding. Cf. Wei, *Exposition*, 106ff.; and R. Wilhelm, *I Ching*, 356–65, esp. 721–23.

64. Cited in R. Smith, *Fortune-tellers and Philosophers*, 112. Most of the following material on *Yijing* divination is drawn from this source, 112–19, which cites several stories from Jonathan Spence's *Emperor of China*, 30, 44ff.

65. Lynn, *Classic of Changes*, 267; cf. R. Wilhelm, *I Ching*, 87, 492.

66. Lynn, *Classic of Changes*, 269–70; cf. R Wilhelm, *I Ching*, 88, 493.

67. Lynn, *Classic of Changes*, 495, slightly modified; cf. R. Wilhelm, *I Ching*, 217, 676.

68. Lynn, *Classic of Changes*, 139, slightly modified; cf. R. Wilhelm, *I Ching*, 9, 383.

69. Lynn, *Classic of Changes*, 487, slightly modified; cf. R. Wilhelm, *I Ching*, 213, 670.

70. Ibid. (both sources).

71. R. Wilhelm, *I Ching*, 215, 672–73. Lynn, *Classic of Changes*, 490, offers a significantly different reading of this line—one shaded by earlier understandings of the text.

72. Lynn, *Classic of Changes*, 407–8, slightly modified. Cf. R. Wilhelm, *I Ching*, 168–70, 605–7.

73. Again, the following discussion is drawn primarily from R. Smith, *Fortune-tellers and Philosophers*, 115–19.

74. Lynn, *Classic of Changes*, 351; cf. R. Wilhelm, *I Ching*, 136–39, 559–63.
75. Lynn, *Classic of Changes*, 357–62; cf. R. Wilhelm, *I Ching*, 139–42, 564–69.
76. Lynn, *Classic of Changes*, 481–82; cf. R. Wilhelm, *I Ching*, 208–12, 663–68.
77. On Tai and Pi, respectively, see Lynn, *Classic of Changes*, 205–15; cf. R. Wilhelm, *I Ching*, 48–55, 440–50. On the second line of Qian, see Lynn, *Classic of Changes*, 133, esp. 384–85; cf. R. Wilhelm, *I Ching*, 8, 380.
78. Cited in R. Smith, *Fortune-tellers and Philosophers*, 118.
79. Ibid.

PART TWO The Transnational Travels of the *Yijing*
1. For some useful works on the transnational travels of texts and ideas, see Damrosch, *What Is World Literature?*; Hofmeyer, *The Portable Bunyan*; Batchelor, *Awakening of the West*; Coleman, *New Buddhism;* and J. J. Clark, *Tao of the West*.
2. See Barbara Herrnstein Smith quoted in Damrosch, *What Is World Literature?*, 8.
3. This is the argument of Damrosch, *What Is World Literature?*.
4. Quoted in ibid., 7. See also the discussion in Knechtges, "Perils and Pleasures."

CHAPTER 4 The *Changes* in East Asia
1. For an excellent basic summary of similarities and differences in the reception and use of Confucian ideas in these environments, see Elman, Duncan, and

Ooms, eds, *Rethinking Confucianism*, 1–29; cf. Tu and Tucker, eds, *Confucian Spirituality*, 183–319; and Kelly, "Vietnam" and "'Confucianism.'"

2. See the introduction to Elman, Duncan, and Ooms, eds., *Rethinking Confucianism*, 4.

3. See Makoto in ibid., 378ff.

4. See Duncan in ibid., 67–68 and 72–94, esp. 76–88.

5. See Woodside in ibid., 127–34; Taylor in ibid., 343–46; and McHale in ibid., 404. Cf. Kelly, "'Confucianism.'"

6. See Benjamin Wai-ming Ng's *The I Ching in Tokugawa Thought and Culture*, based on his even more expansive dissertation, "Hollyhock and the Hexagrams." I would like to acknowledge here an enormous personal and professional debt to Professor Ng, who has pioneered in the study of the *Changes* and its travels in East Asia—not only Japan but also Korea and Vietnam.

7. Ng, *I Ching*, 66–67.

8. Ibid., 60. Cf. Lynn, *Classic of Changes*, 106.

9. Ibid., 68, modified. For this line, see Lynn, *Classic of Changes*, 138–39; cf. R. Wilhelm, *I Ching*, 9–10, 383–85.

10. Ng, *I Ching*, 116. For this quotation, see Lynn, *Classic of Changes*, 52; cf. R. Wilhelm, *I Ching*, 294.

11. Ng, *I Ching*, 98. For this quotation, see Lynn, *Classic of Changes*, 260, modified; cf. R. Wilhelm, *I Ching*, 486.

12. Ng, *I Ching*, 100, modified.

13. Ng, "Hollyhock and the Hexagrams," 338–80, includes a breakdown of Japanese writings in the Tokugawa period by author, subject, and intellectual orientation.

14. See Ng, *I Ching*, 24, 40; also Shchutskii, *Researches*, 47, 61–62, and 113–18.

15. For details, see Tucker, "From Nativism to Numerology."

16. These points are abundantly documented in Ng, *I Ching*, esp. 55–205, and "Hollyhock and the Hexagrams."

17. Ng, *I Ching*, 107. I have modified this translation somewhat and patched two disconnected but related passages together.

18. Ibid., 109–10.

19. Ng, *I Ching*, 39–40, 57–58, and 120–21, esp. 58, modified. For this passage, see Lynn, *Classic of Changes*, 449; cf. R. Wilhelm, *I Ching*, 192, 640.

20. Ng, *I Ching*, 71–72.

21. Ibid., 75–77, esp. 76, modified.

22. See, for example, Yoon, *Culture of Fengshui*.

23. See Fendos, *"Book of Changes"*; and Ng, "Hollyhock and the Hexagrams," esp. 417–37. Note also the many relevant essays in de Bary and Haboush, eds., *The Rise of Neo-Confucianism in Korea*.

24. See Ng, "Late Chosŏn Thought," 54–55; also Choi, *Modern History*, 50–64.

25. See Yun, *Critical Issues;* and the summary in Choi, *Modern History*, 67–81.

26. For T'oegye's disagreements with Zhu Xi and T'oegye's changing philosophical opinions, see Tomoeda, "Yi T'oegye," in de Bary and Haboush, *Rise of Neo-Confucianism*, 243–60.

27. See ibid.; Ng, "Late Chosŏn Thought," 56; see also Kalton, et al., trans., *The Four-Seven Debate*; and Kalton, trans., *To Become a Sage*.

28. Ng, "Late Chosŏn Thought," 56–57; Choi, *Modern History*, 84–101, esp. 89 and 90nn137, 138 (Korean text). Cf. Lynn, *Classic of Changes*, 67; and R. Wilhelm, *I Ching*, 321–23.

29. Ro, *Korean Neo-Confucianism*, 90–92.

30. See Choi, *Modern History*, 101–7, esp. 105n170 (Korean text).

31. Ng, "Late Chosŏn Thought," 58.

32. Although I am in general agreement with Ng's conclusions in "Late Chosŏn Thought," esp. 65, based on my own research I believe that Korean *Yijing* studies in the Choson period were both more important philosophically and more eclectic than he suggests.

33. These and the following remarks on Chang's *Illustrated Explanation of Changes Scholarship* are based primarily on my own research in the Kyujanggak Archives of Seoul University, inspired by Yung Sik Kim's "Western Science."

34. Ng, "Late Chosŏn Thought," 59.

35. See the excellent summary of Yi's and especially Chong's ideas in Ng, "Late Chosŏn Thought," 59–63; also Ng's dissertation, "Hollyhock and the Hexagrams," 429–33. J. Lee, "*Book of Change*," 15, discusses Chong's methods of hexagram interpretation.

36. See Yung Sik Kim, "Science," 127–29; also Ng, "Hollyhock and the Hexagrams," 432–34. Chong believed that Zheng's theories encouraged people to engage in "base practices" such as geomancy, physiognomy, fate extrapolation, and the choice of auspicious days, which only misled them.

37. See Ng, "Late Chosŏn Thought," 63; and Yung Sik Kim, "Science," 134. Kim and Setton, *Chong Yagyong*,

provide exceptionally valuable studies of the complexity of Chong's worldview.

38. See Ng, "Late Chosŏn Thought," 64.

39. See Fendos, *"Book of Changes,"* 55–58.

40. Sin argued, on the basis of forged texts, that Fuxi was in fact a Korean prince who had learned the *Changes* from Hang Wong, an early Hangguk ruler. Ng, "Hollyhock and the Hexagrams," 436n55.

41. For details, see Lee, "Origin," esp. 229ff.; also Fendos, *"Book of Changes,"* 56ff. Kim's intent was to internationalize the *Yijing*. See Lee, "Origin," 237.

42. Lee, "Origin," 234ff.

43. Fendos, *"Book of Changes,"* 55–58.

44. See Kelly, "Vietnam" and "'Confucianism.'"

45. See Ng, *"Yijing* Scholarship," 2–3.

46. For an excellent description of Great One numerology, see Ho, *Chinese Mathematical Astrology*, 42–68.

47. Nguyen is also one of the three main "saints" of the Cao Dai religion, together with Victor Hugo and Sun Yat-sen (see below).

48. See Woodside in Elman, Duncan, and Ooms, eds, *Rethinking*, 116–43.

49. See Ng, *"Yijing* Scholarship."

50. See the discussion in ibid., 3.

51. See, for example, ibid., 5.

52. These remarks on *Yijing*-related manuscripts in Vietnam are based primarily on my research notes from the Hanoi National Library.

53. The original poem is included but not translated in Tran, *Vietnamese Scholar*, appendix C, "Poems in Chinese."

54. Ng, "*Yijing* Scholarship," 4ff., discusses Le's writings at considerable length.

55. Cited in ibid., 7, slightly modified.

56. Ibid., 11, slightly modified. Le was also sharply critical of both Christianity and the idea of social equality. Ibid., 13–14.

57. Dickinson and Moore, "Trigrams," esp. 41–47. Thuken's teacher, Changkya Rolpai Dorjé (1717–86), is known to have written commentaries on the *Yijing*, but I have been unable to find any copies.

58. See Thuken, *Crystal Mirror*, 331–49, esp. 335–37.

59. Cornu, *Astrology*, 102–26, discusses *mewa* and the eight trigrams at considerable length. Dickinson and Moore, "Trigrams," 17–22, identify interesting parallels with Chinese geomantic conceptions in the movement of numbers within the *mewa*.

60. Cf. the discussion in Cornu, *Astrology*, esp. 102–26. The "white beryl" metaphor refers to the "crystal clarity of predictions based on astrology and divination." Dorje, *Tibetan Elemental Divination Paintings*, 402n26.

61. Dorje, *Tibetan Elemental Divination Paintings*, 20.

62. Ibid., 21, 345ff.; cf. Cornu, *Astrology*, 101.

63. Dorje, *Tibetan Elemental Divination Paintings*, 21; cf. the discussion in Cornu, *Astrology*, 41–46, 253–57.

64. Astrology was studied as part of the medical curriculum in Tibet; see Cornu, *Astrology*, 15–17, 49–84; cf. "Foreword" to Dorje, *Tibetan Elemental Divination Paintings*, 11–21.

65. Cornu, *Astrology*, 174–215.

66. Ibid., 216–44.

67. Dickinson and Moore, "Trigrams," esp. 3, 41–43. See also Dorje, *Tibetan Elemental Divination Paintings*, 402n18; and Thuken, *Crystal Mirror*, 337.

68. Dickinson and Moore, "Trigrams," 41–43; Dorje, *Tibetan Elemental Divination Paintings*, 106.

69. Note also the divinatory significance of different "pairings" (juxtapositions) of the eight trigrams, as discussed in Cornu, *Astrology*, 120–26, esp. 123.

70. Ibid., 107–18. Dorje, *Tibetan Elemental Divination Paintings*, 106ff., discusses at length the distinctive ways eight trigrams were interpreted in Tibet. See also Cammann, "The Eight Trigrams," esp. 313ff. Recall that the Chinese solution to the problem of correlation was to associate some agents with more than one trigram.

71. See Cornu, *Astrology*; Dickinson and Moore, "Trigrams"; Dorje, Gyatso, *Tibetan Elemental Divination Paintings*.

72. Ng, "Divination and Meiji Politics," discusses Takashima's fascinating career. For the English translation of Takashima's book, which contains a great many examples of his divinations, see Takashima, *Takashima Ekidan*.

73. See R. Smith, *Fathoming the Cosmos*, chap. 8, for these and other examples of the trend.

74. Unlike the two standard Chinese configurations, these trigrams are arrayed counterclockwise in Cao Dai temples, with the Dui trigram in the west, Qian in the southwest, Kan in the south, Gen in the southeast, Zhen in the east, Sun in the northeast, Li in the north, and Kun in the northwest.

75. See Le, *Three Teachings*. For a convenient view from inside the faith, consult http://english.caodai.net/; also http://www.caodai.org.

CHAPTER 5 The Westward Travels of the *Changes*

1. See, for example, Batchelor, *Awakening of the West*, xi.
2. Many scholars have insightfully explored these problems of translation. See, for example, Knechtges, "Perils and Pleasures," which focuses primarily on the *Yijing*.
3. This section on the Jesuits has been drawn largely from R. Smith, "Jesuit Interpretations." See also Claudia von Collani's excellent study, "First Encounter."
4. See von Collani, "First Encounter," 239ff., esp. 253–56.
5. Cited in R. Smith, "Jesuit Interpretations."
6. Ibid., 39. "Sap." refers here to the "apocryphal" work known as *Liber Sapientiae* or "Book of Wisdom."
7. A thorough analysis of this diagram can be found in R. Smith, "Jesuit Interpretations."
8. For details, see ibid. and von Collani, "First Encounter."
9. For details of the correspondence between Bouvet and Leibniz, see von Collani, "First Encounter," 241–43.
10. Bouvet and Leibniz took the liberty of calculating the numbers of each hexagram line from the top down rather than from the bottom up, as in the Chinese fashion.
11. Cf. Ryan, "Leibniz," 65–67, 78ff.
12. Von Collani, "First Encounter," 238, 275ff., compares this rendering with other Christian interpretations of the Qian hexagram.
13. The invidious reference here is to Bouvet's claim

that Fuxi was the Old Testament patriarch Henoch (Enoch), and that the *Yijing* was a fragment of the "Apocalypse of Henoch."

14. This account of the translation project is drawn primarily from von Collani, "First Encounter," 258ff.

15. Ibid., 266–75, provides a detailed content analysis of this work. See also ibid., 313 ff., for de Mailla's Latin translations of selected wings of the *Changes*.

16. For an overview of various Western translations of the *Changes*, including the ones mentioned above, consult Rutt, *Zhouyi*, 60–82; and Shchutskii, *Researches*, 13–55.

17. Girardot, *Victorian*, 371–72. Helena Petrovna Blavatsky (1831–1891) was one of the founders of the Theosophy movement, which influenced later exponents of the *Changes*, including Aleister Crowley, discussed below.

18. Philastre's work was republished by Maisonneuve (Paris, 1982) and then reissued in a single volume by Editions Zulma (Paris, 1992), with a preface by the renowned French scholar François Jullien.

19. Rutt, *Zhouyi*, 71–72, provides overviews of, and brief excerpts from, both works.

20. R. Smith, "Jesuit Interpretations," 29.

21. Cited in ibid.

22. See Shaughnessy, *I Ching*, 17. Cf. Shchutskii, *Researches*, 23–24.

23. On Legge's translation of the *Changes*, see Girardot, *Victorian*, esp. 366–74.

24. He did, however, insist that the Chinese term Di (or Shangdi)—lit., "Lord on High"—should be rendered "God." See the discussion in ibid., 372–73.

25. Legge, *I Ching*, xvii.

26. Ibid., xiv–xv, 10, 17, 25–26, 38, etc.

27. For details, see Hon, "Constancy in Change."

28. Kingsmill, "Review," 92.

29. Edkins, "The *Yi King* of the Chinese" and "*Yi King* with Notes." The quotation is from the latter, 425.

30. Terrien de LaCouperie, "Oldest Book," 15:237–47, 254–59.

31. Ibid., 15:248–51; 14:781–83n3.

32. Ibid., 15:252ff, esp. 262.

33. Ibid., esp. 277ff. A Jesuit priest, Niccolo Longobardo (1565–1655), once asserted that Fuxi was Zoroaster, the king of Bactria, whose powers as the discoverer of magic invested the trigrams with their special potency.

34. Shchutskii, *Researches*, 24–27.

35. Rutt, *Zhouyi*, 60–82, provides a useful summary of various translations of the *Changes* into European languages.

36. See Gerald Swanson's introduction to Shchutskii, *Researches*, xi–xii. For an excellent, historically sensitive analysis of these two works, see Tze-ki Hon's "Constancy in Change." Shchutskii's evaluation of Wilhelm's work appears in *Researches on the I Ching*, 37–46. For his amusing general summary of European interpretations of the *Changes*, see ibid., 55.

37. See the discussion in R. Smith, "Key Concepts," 30–32. The Vatican Archives contain a copy of this work, which was obviously used by the Jesuit missionaries in China—quite possibly Bouvet, Fouquet, or both.

38. See Lackner, "Richard Wilhelm."

39. Ibid.

40. Cornelius and Cornelius, "*Yi King*," esp. 19ff.

41. Ibid., 21. For a similar effort to link the *Yijing* to the kabbala, see Charlie Higgins, "The Hexagram and the Kabbalah," http://www.mension.com/del_3.htm (1997).

42. Eason, *I Ching Divination*, 15.

43. See "Translations of Hexagram Names," http://chaocenter.rice.edu/Content.aspx?id=601; "Some Western-Language Works on the *Yijing*," http://www.aasianst.org/eaa/smith.htm; and the book reviews at http://www.biroco.com/Yijing/reviews.htm. For some examples of recent Western-language scholarship on the *Changes*, see Cheng, ed., "Philosophy of the Yi" and "The *Yijing* and Its Commentaries"; also R. Smith, "Select Bibliography."

44. Gardner, "Confucian Commentary," 416–17.

45. For updates to the work by Hacker, Moore, and Patsco, see "*I-Ching* Bookmarks," http://www.zhouyi.com. This site also includes information on non-English resources.

46. See Capra, *Tao of Physics*, esp. 108–10, 278–83.

47. Kripal, *Easlen*, 302–7, 314.

48. Capra, "Where Have all the Flowers Gone?" (n.p.).

49. McKenna and McKenna, *Invisible Landscape*, chaps. 8 and 9. For an illuminating biography of Terrence McKenna, see Kripal, *Easlen*, 368–76.

50. R. Wilhelm, *I Ching*, xxxiv.

51. See Jung, *Man and His Symbols*, 356–60.

52. For Nathan Sivins's review of Blofeld's translation, in which Sivins explicitly compares it with Wilhelm's

I Ching, see the *Harvard Journal of Asiatic Studies* 26 (1966): 290–98.

53. See http://www.interferenza.com/bcs/interw/65-nov26.htm.

54. See http://www.songmeanings.net/songs/view/3530822107858787624/.

55. See, for example, Dick, *Man in the High Castle*, 12–13.

56. Debon, *Doukiplèdonktan?*, esp. 155ff.

57. Sheringham, *Everyday Life*, 349.

58. For the original version in French, see Andrews, "Numerology and Mathematics," 297.

59. This analysis follows ibid., 298.

60. Cited in Moore, "*Yijing* in Mexico," 3. Much of the following material comes from this excellent unpublished paper.

61. Tae, *La Presencia del Yijing*, 261.

62. In 1982 Serrano would publish *Libro de Hexaedros* (Book of Hexadrons), a collection of sixty-four poems that together reinterpreted and synthesized images and processes that were reflected in the hexagrams of the *Changes*.

63. Tae, "*Yijing* y Creación Poetica," 14–18.

64. Cage, *Silence*, "About the Author." Rockwell also opined that "the entire American avante-garde would be unthinkable without Cage's music, writings, and genially patriarchical personality." Ibid.

65. Ibid., 60–61.

66. See Marshall, "John Cage's *I Ching* Chance Operations." The title of the play, *Marrying Maiden,* comes from Wilhelm's translation of the name of hexagram number 54.

67. Cage, "Tokyo Lecture," 7.

68. Tenney, *Silence*, 64–65.

69. Ibid., 66–87, is full of extraordinarily complex charts, mathematical equations, and discussions of harmonics.

70. The literature on both these topics is vast. For instance, a Google search using the term "fengshui" on August 17, 2010, yielded 10.2 million results.

CONCLUDING REMARKS

1. R. Smith, *Fathoming the Cosmos*, 241–49, offers some comparisons along these lines.

2. See, for example, ibid., esp. chap. 9; also "The *Changes* as a Mirror of the Mind," "The *Yijing* in Global Perspective," "Jesuit Interpretations," and so forth.

3. For a detailed description of the ideal prototype, which consists of thirty-eight rings, see Feuchtwang, *Anthropological Analysis*, esp. 37–67.

4. Cited in R. Smith, *Fortune-tellers and Philosophers*, 123.

5. See also Legge, *I Ching*, 38.

6. See R. Smith, *Fathoming the Cosmos*, 141, 184–86, 193, and 240. The quotation has been slightly modified.

7. See Needham, *Science and Civilisation*, 2:292, 304–40; 3:56–59, 119–20, 140–41, 464, 625; 4.1:14, 16; 4.2:143, 530; 4.3:125; 5.3: 51–53, 60–66, 69–74, 128, 201, 217.

8. Yang, *Book of Changes*, esp. chaps. 6–13. See also Zhang, "*Book of Changes*."

9. Ho, "System of the *Book of Changes*," esp. 38. Cf. Needham, *Science and Civilisation*, 2:336; and 7.2:125–27.

10. See Unschuld, *Medicine in China*, 57–58; see also 79, 85–86, and 194ff., esp. 215–28.

11. See R. Smith, "The *Changes* as a Mirror of the Mind."

12. Yang, *Book of Changes*, 296–300.

13. See R. Smith, *Fathoming the Cosmos*, 208–11.

Bibliography

Note: In the interest of space, this bibliography includes only the Western-language works that are cited in the notes.

Adler, Joseph. *Introduction to the Study of the Classic of Change (I-hsüeh ch'i-meng)*. New York: Global Scholarly Publications, 2002.

Andrews, Chris. "Numerology and Mathematics in the Writing of Raymond Queneau." *Forum for Modern Language Studies* 40.3 (July 2004): 291–300.

Batchelor, Stephen. *The Awakening of the West: The Encounter of Buddhism and Western Culture.* Berkeley: Parallax Press, 1994.

Birdwhistell, Anne. *Transition to Neo-Confucianism: Shao Yung on Knowledge and Symbols of Reality.* Stanford: Stanford University Press, 1989.

Cage, John. *Silence: Lectures and Writings.* Middletown, CT: Wesleyan University, 1961.

———. "Tokyo Lecture and Three Mesostics." *Perspectives of New Music* 26.1 (Winter 1988): 6–25.

Cammann, Schuyler. "The Eight Trigrams: Variants and Their Uses." *History of Religions* 29.4 (May 1990): 301–17.

————. "Some Early Chinese Symbols of Duality." *History of Religions* 24.3 (1985): 215–54.

Capra, Fritjof. *The Tao of Physics: An Exploration of the Parallels between Modern Physics and Eastern Mysticism.* Boston: Shambala Publications, 1975.

————. "Where Have All the Flowers Gone? Reflections on the Spirit and Legacy of the Sixties." 2002. http://www.fritjofcapra.net/articles120102.html.

Chan, Wing-tsit, ed. *Chu Hsi and Neo-Confucianism.* Honolulu: University of Hawaii Press, 1986.

Cheng, Chung-ying, ed. "Philosophy of the *Yi*: Unity and Dialectics." Special edition of the *Journal of Chinese Philosophy* 36.1 (December 2009): 1–163.

————, ed. "The *Yijing* and Its Commentaries." Special edition of the *Journal of Chinese Philosophy* 35.2 (June 2008): 191–375.

Choi, Min-Hong. *A Modern History of Korean Philosophy.* Seoul: Seong Moon Sa, 1980.

Clark, J. J. *The Tao of the West: Western Transformations of Taoist Thought.* London: Routledge, 2000.

Cleary, Thomas. *The Buddhist I Ching.* Boston: Shambala, 2001.

————. *The Taoist I Ching.* Boston: Shambala, 2005.

Coleman, James W. *The New Buddhism: The Western Transformation of an Ancient Tradition.* Oxford: Oxford University Press, 2001.

Collani, Claudia von. "The First Encounter of the West with the *Yijing*: Introduction to and Edition of Letters and Latin Translations by French Jesuits from the 18th Century." *Monumenta Serica* 55 (2007): 227–387.

Cook, Richard S. *Classical Chinese Combinatorics: Derivation of the Book of Changes Hexagram Sequence.*

Berkeley: Sino-Tibetan Etymological Dictionary and
Thesaurus Project, 2006.

Cornelius, J. Edward, and Marlene Cornelius, eds. "*Yi King*: A Beastly Book of Changes." *Red Flame* 5 (1998): 1–122.

Cullen, Christopher. "The Science/Technology Interface in Seventeenth-Century China: Song Yingxing on '*Qi*' and the '*Wuxing*.'" *Bulletin of the School of Oriental and African Studies* 53.2 (1990): 295–318.

Damrosch, David. *What Is World Literature?* Princeton: Princeton University Press, 2003.

de Bary, W. T., and Irene Bloom, eds. *Sources of Chinese Tradition.* Volume 1. New York: Columbia University Press, 1999.

de Bary, W. T., and JaHyun Kim Haboush, eds. *The Rise of Neo-Confucianism in Korea.* New York: Columbia University Press, 1985.

Debon, Claude. *Doukiplèdonktan?: études sur Raymond Queneau.* Paris: Presses de la Sorbonne nouvelle, 1997.

Dick, Philip K. *The Man in the High Castle.* New York: Vintage Books, 1992.

Dickinson, Gary, and Steve Moore. "Trigrams and Tortoises: Sino-Tibetan Divination." Special issue of *Oracle* 1.5 (Summer 1997): 1–48.

Ding, Zijiang. "The Numerical Mysticism of Shao Yong and Pythagoras." *Journal of Chinese Philosophy* 32.4 (December 2005): 615–32.

Dorje, Gyurme, ed. *Tibetan Elemental Divination Paintings: Illuminated Manuscripts from The White Beryl of Sangs-rgyas rGya-mtsho, with the Moonbeams Treatise of Lo-chen Dharmaśrī.* London: John Eskenazi and Sam Fogg, 2001.

Edkins, Joseph. "The *Yi King* of the Chinese, as a Book of Divination." *Journal of the Royal Asiatic Society* n.s. 16 (1884): 360–80.

———. "The *Yi King*, with Notes on the 64 Kwa." *China Review* 12 (1883–84): 77–88, 412–32.

Elman, Benjamin A., John B. Duncan, and Herman Ooms, eds. *Rethinking Confucianism: Past and Present in China, Japan, Korea, and Vietnam*. Los Angeles: UCLA Asian Pacific Monograph Series, 2002.

Fendos, Paul G., Jr. "*Book of Changes* Studies in Korea." *Asian Studies Review* 23.1 (March 1999): 49–68.

Feuchtwang, Stephan. *An Anthropological Analysis of Chinese Geomancy*. Bangkok: White Lotus Press, 2002.

Field, Stephen L. *Ancient Chinese Divination*. Honolulu: University of Hawaii Press, 2008.

Gardner, Daniel K. "Confucian Commentary and Chinese Intellectual History." *Journal of Asian Studies* 57.2 (1998): 397–422.

Girardot, Norman J. *The Victorian Translation of China: James Legge's Oriental Pilgrimage*. Berkeley: University of California Press, 2002.

Goodman, Howard L. "Exegetes and Exegesis of the *Book of Changes* in the Third Century A.D.: Historical and Scholastic Contexts for Wang Pi." Ph.D. dissertation, Princeton University, 1985. Available from UMI Dissertation Services/ProQuest.

Gotshalk, Richard. *Divination, Order, and the Zhouyi*. Lanham, MD: University Press of America, 1999.

Granet, Marcel. *La Pensée chinoise*. Paris: Editions Albin Michel, 1968 (electronic edition by Pierre Palpant; originally published in 1934).

Hacker, Edward, Steve Moore, and Lorraine Patsco, eds. *I Ching: An Annotated Bibliography*. London: Taylor and Francis, 2002. For updates, see "I-Ching Bookmarks," http://www.zhouyi.com/.

Hall, David L., and Roger T. Ames. *Anticipating China: Thinking through the Narratives of Chinese and Western Culture*. Albany: State University of New York Press, 1995.

Ho, Peng Yoke. *Chinese Mathematical Astrology: Reaching Out to the Stars*. New York: RoutledgeCurzon, 2003.

———. "The System of the *Book of Changes* and Chinese Science." *Japanese Studies in the History of Science* 11 (1972): 23–39.

Hofmeyer, Isabel. *The Portable Bunyan: A Transnational History of The Pilgrim's Progress*. Princeton: Princeton University Press, 2004.

Hon, Tze-ki. "Constancy in Change: A Comparison of James Legge's and Richard Wilhelm's Interpretations of the *Yijing*." *Monumental Serica* 53 (2005): 315–36.

———. "Hexagrams and Politics: Wang Bi's Political Philosophy in the *Zhouyi zhu*." In *Ethics, Religion, and the World of Thought in Early Medieval China*, edited by Alan Chan and Yuet-keung Lo. Albany: State University of New York Press, 2008.

———. "Human Agency and Change: A Reading of Wang Bi's *Yijing* Commentary." *Journal of Chinese Philosophy* 30.2 (June 2003): 223–42.

———. *The Yijing and Chinese Politics: Classical Commentary and Literati Activism in the Northern Song Period, 960–1127*. Albany: State University of New York Press, 2005.

Jullien, François, ed. *Le Yi king: Traduit du chinois par*

Paul-Louis-Félix Philastre et présenté par François
Jullien. Paris: Zulma, 2006.

Jung, Carl G. *Man and His Symbols*. London: Aldus
Books, 1964.

Kalton, Michael C., trans. *To Become a Sage: The Ten
Diagrams on Sage Learning by Yi T'oegye*. New York:
Columbia University Press, 1988.

Kalton, Michael C., et al., trans. *The Four-Seven Debate: An
Annotated Translation of the Most Famous Controversy
in Korean Neo-Confucian Thought*. Albany: State
University of New York Press, 1994.

Kang, C. H., and Ethel R. Nelson. *The Discovery of Genesis:
How the Truths of Genesis Were Found Hidden in the
Chinese Language*. St. Louis: Concordia, 1979.

Keightley, David. *Sources of Shang History: The Oracle-Bone
Inscriptions of Bronze Age China*. 2nd ed. Berkeley:
University of California Press, 1985.

Kelly, Liam. "'Confucianism' in Vietnam: A State of the
Field Essay." *Journal of Vietnamese Studies*, 1.1–2
(2006): 314–70.

———. "Vietnam as a 'Domain of Manifest Civility.'"
Journal of Southeast Asian Studies 34.1 (February
2003): 63–76.

Kim, Yung Sik. "Science and the Confucian Tradition in
the Work of Chong Yagyong." *Tasanhak* 5 (June
2004): 127–68.

———. "Western Science, Cosmological Ideas, and the
Yijing Studies in Seventeenth- and Eighteenth-Cen-
tury Korea." *Seoul Journal of Korean Studies* 14
(December 2001): 299–334.

Kingsmill, Thomas. "Review of Volume 16 of Sacred Books

of the East." *China Review* 11.2 (November 1882): 86–92.

Knechtges, David R. "The Perils and Pleasures of Translation: The Case of the Chinese Classics." *Selected Papers of the Center for Zhouyi and Ancient Chinese Philosophy* (October 2006). http://zhouyi.sdu.edu.cn/english/newsxitong/selectedPapers/2006101194856.htm.

Kripal, Jeffrey J. *Easlen: America and the Religion of No Religion*. Chicago: University of Chicago Press, 2007.

Kunst, Richard A. "The Original *Yijing*: A Text, Phonetic Transcription, Translation, and Indexes, with Sample Glosses." Ph.D. dissertation, University of California, Berkeley, 1985. Available from UMI Dissertation Services/ProQuest.

Lackner, Michael. "Richard Wilhelm: A 'Sinicized' German Translator." In *De l'un au multiple. La traduction du chinois dans les langues européennes*, edited by Viviane Alleton and Michael Lackner. Paris: Maison des Science de l'Homme, 1998.

Le, Anh Minh. *The Three Teachings of Vietnam as an Ideological Precondition for the Foundation of Caodaism*. San Martin, CA: Tam Giao Dong Nguyen Publishing House, 1910. http://www.tamgiaodongnguyen.com/Books/TamGiaoVietNam-web.pdf.

Lee, Jung Young. "The *Book of Change* and Korean Thought." In *Religions in Korea: Beliefs and Cultural Values*, edited by Earl H. Phillips and Eui-young Yu. Los Angeles: Center for Korean-American and Korean Studies, California State University, Los Angeles, 1982.

———. *Embracing Change: Postmodern Interpretations of the I Ching from a Christian Perspective.* Scranton: University of Scranton Press, 1994.

———. "The Origin and Significance of the *Chongyok* or Book of Correct Change." *Journal of Chinese Philosophy* 9 (1982): 211–41.

Legge, James. *The I Ching* [originally rendered *Yi King*]. New York: Dover Publications, 1963 (reprint of 1899 edition).

Lo, Yuet Keung. "Change beyond Syncretism: Ouyi Zhixu's Buddhist Hermeneutics of the *Yijing*." *Journal of Chinese Philosophy* 35.2 (June 2008): 273–95.

Lynn, Richard John. *The Classic of Changes: A New Translation of the I Ching as Interpreted by Wang Bi.* New York: Columbia University Press, 1994.

MacGillivray, D. "A New Interpretation of the Book of Changes." *Chinese Recorder* 47 (May 1918): 310–16.

Marshall, S. J. "John Cage's *I Ching* Change Operations." http://www.biroco.com/yijing/cage.htm.

———. *The Mandate of Heaven: Hidden History in the I Ching.* New York: Columbia University Press, 2001.

McCaffree, Joseph E. *Bible and I Ching Relationships.* Hong Kong: South Sky Book Co., 1982.

McKenna, Terence, and Dennis McKenna. *The Invisible Landscape: Mind, Hallucinogens, and the I Ching.* New York: Seabury Press, 1975; republished in 1993 by HarperCollins.

Meyer, Andrew Seth. "The Correct Meaning of the Five Classics and the Intellectual Foundations of the Tang." Ph.D. dissertation, Harvard University, 1999. Available from UMI Dissertation Services/ ProQuest.

Meyer, A., Robert Weller, and Peter Bol. "Cosmic Reso-
    nance Theory." http://isites.harvard.edu/fs/docs/icb
    .topic46659.files/Cosmic_Resonance_Theory.htm.
Moore, Naturaleza. "The *Yijing* in Mexico." Ms. (2002):
    1–18.
Needham, Joseph. *Science and Civilisation in China.*
    Multiple vols. Cambridge: Cambridge University
    Press, 1956–.
Ng, Benjamin Wai-ming. "Divination and Meiji Politics: A
    Reading of Takashima Kaemon's Judgments on the
    Book of Changes (Takashima Ekidan)." Paper
    presented at the Conference on Daoist Studies,
    University of British Columbia, October 24–26,
    2008.
———. "The Hollyhocks and the Hexagrams: The *I Ching*
    in Tokugawa Thought and Culture." 2 vols. Ph.D.
    dissertation, Princeton University, 1996. Available
    from UMI Dissertation Services/ProQuest.
———. "The I Ching in Late Chosŏn Thought." *Korean
    Studies* 24 (2000): 53–68.
———. *The I Ching in Tokugawa Thought and Culture.*
    Honolulu: University of Hawaii Press, 2000.
———. "*Yijing* Scholarship in Late-Nguyen Vietnam: A
    Study of Le Van Ngu's *Chu Dich Cuu Nguyen* (An
    Investigation of the Origins of the *Yijing*, 1916)."
    Review of Vietnamese Studies 3.1 (December 2003):
    1–14.
Nielsen, Bent. *A Companion to Yi jing Numerology and
    Cosmology: Chinese Studies of Images and Numbers
    from Han (202 BCE–220 CE) to Song (960–1279 CE).*
    London: RoutledgeCurzon, 2003.
Peterson, Willard. "Making Connections: 'Commentary

on the Attached Verbalizations' of the *Book of Change.*" *Harvard Journal of Asiatic Studies* 42 (1982): 67–116.

Pregadio, Fabrizio. *Great Clarity: Daoism and Alchemy in Early Medieval China.* Stanford: Stanford University Press, 2006

Roth, Harold D. "Psychology and Self-Cultivation in Early Chinese Thought." *Harvard Journal of Asiatic Studies* 51.2 (December 1991): 599–650.

Rutt, Richard. *The Book of Changes (Zhouyi).* Richmond, Surrey: Curzon Press, 1996.

Ryan, James A. "Leibniz's Binary System and Shao Yong's *Yijing.*" *Philosophy East and West* 46.1 (1996): 59–90.

Schilling, Dennis R. *Yijing. Das Buch der Wandlungen.* Frankfurt: Verlag, 2009.

Setton, Mark. *Chong Yagyong: Korea's Challenge to Orthodox Neo-Confucianism.* Albany: State University of New York Press, 1997.

Shaughnessy, Edward L. "The Composition of the *Zhouyi.*" Ph.D. dissertation, Stanford University, 1983. Available from UMI Dissertation Services/ProQuest.

———. *I Ching: The Classic of Changes.* New York: Ballantine Books, 1996.

———. "Marriage, Divorce and Revolution: Reading between the Lines of the *Book of Changes.*" *Journal of Asian Studies* 51.3 (August 1992): 587–99.

Shchutskii, Iulian. *Researches on the I Ching,* translated by William MacDonald and Tsuyoshi Hasegawa. Princeton: Princeton University Press, 1979.

Sheringham, Michael. *Everyday Life: Theories and Practices from Surrealism to the Present.* Oxford: Oxford University Press, 2006.

Smith, Kidder A., ed. *Sung Dynasty Uses of the I Ching*. Princeton: Princeton University Press, 1990.

——. "*Zhouyi* Divination from Accounts in the *Zuozhuan*." *Harvard Journal of Asiatic Studies* 49.2 (1989): 424–63.

Smith, Richard J. "The *Changes* as a Mirror of the Mind: The Evolution of the *Zhouyi* in China and Beyond." 2009. http://chaocenter.rice.edu/Content. aspx?id=601.

——. "Divination in Late Imperial China: New Light on Some Old Problems." In *The Imperative of Understanding: Chinese Philosophy, Comparative Philosophy, and Onto-Hermeneutics*, edited by On-cho Ng, 273–315. New York: Global Scholarly Publications, 2008.

——. *Fathoming the Cosmos and Ordering the World: The Yijing (I-Ching, or Classic of Changes) and Its Evolution in China*. Charlottesville: University of Virginia Press, 2008. Online glossaries available at http:// chaocenter.rice.edu/Content.aspx?id=601.

——. *Fortune-tellers and Philosophers: Divination in Traditional Chinese Society*. Boulder: Westview Press, 1991.

——. "Jesuit Interpretations of the *Yijing* (Classic of Changes) in Historical and Comparative Perspective." 2003. http://chaocenter.rice.edu/Content. aspx?id=601.

——. "Select Bibliography of Works on the *Yijing* since 1985." *Journal of Chinese Philosophy* 36.1 (December 2009): 152–163.

——. "The *Yijing* (*Classic of Changes*) in Global Perspective: Some Reflections." 2002. http://chaocenter.rice .edu/Content.aspx?id=601.

Spence, Jonathan. *Emperor of China: Self-Portrait of K'ang-hsi*. New York: Vintage Books, 1988.

Tae, Joung Kwon. "*I Ching* y Creación Poetica." *Vuelta* 229 (1995): 14–18.

———. *La Presencia del I Ching en la Obra de Octavio Paz, Salvador Elizondo y José Agustín*. Guadalajara, Mexico: University of Guadalajara Press, 1998.

Takashima, Kaemon. *The Takashima Ekidan*, translated by Sugiura Shigetake. Tokyo: Keigyosha, 1893.

Terrien de LaCouperie, Albert Étienne Jean-Baptiste. "The Oldest Book of the Chinese: The *Yh-King* and Its Authors." *Journal of the Royal Asiatic Society* 14 (1882): 781–815; 15 (1883): 237–89. Terrien's book with the same title was published in London by D. Nutt in 1892.

Tran, My Van. *A Vietnamese Scholar in Anguish: Nguyen Khuyen and the Decline of the Confucian Order, 1884–1909*. Singapore: National University of Singapore, 1991.

Tu, Weiming, and Mary Evelyn Tucker, eds. *Confucian Spirituality*. 2 vols. New York: Crossroad, 2004.

Tucker, John Allen. "From Nativism to Numerology: Yamaga Soko's Final Excursion into the Metaphysics of Change." *Philosophy East and West* 54.2 (April 2004): 194–217.

Thuken, Losang Chokyi Nyima. *The Crystal Mirror of Philosophical Systems: A Tibetan Study of Asian Religious Thought*, translated by Geshe Lhundub Sopa, edited by Roger R. Jackson. Boston: Wisdom Publications, 2009.

Unschuld, Paul. *Medicine in China: A History of Ideas*.

Berkeley and Los Angeles: University of California Press, 1985.

Wang, Baoxuan. "The Study of Ancient and Modern Text Classics." *Contemporary Chinese Thought* 36.4 (Summer 2005): 58–81.

Wang, Dongliang. *Les signes et les mutations: Une approache nouvelle du Yi King histoire, pratique et texte.* Paris: L'Asiathèque, 1995.

Wang, Shuren, and Lin Zhang. "The Roots of Chinese Philosophy and Culture—An Introduction to 'Xiang' and 'Xiang Thinking.'" *Frontiers of Philosophy in China* 4.1 (March 2009): 1–12.

Wei, Tat. *An Exposition of the I-Ching or Book of Changes.* Hong Kong: Dai Nippon Printing Co., 1977.

Wilhelm, Helmut. "I-Ching Oracles in the *Tso-chuan* and the *Kuo-yü." Journal of the American Oriental Society,* 79.4 (October–December 1959): 275–80.

Wilhelm, Richard, trans. *The I Ching, or Book of Changes,* translated from the German by Cary F. Baynes. Princeton: Princeton University Press, 1967.

Xing, Wen. "Hexagram Pictures and Early *Yi* Schools: Reconsidering the *Book of Changes* in Light of Excavated *Yi* Texts. *Monumenta Serica* 51 (2003): 571–604.

Yang, Li. *Book of Changes and Traditional Chinese Medicine.* Beijing: Beijing Science and Technology Press, 1998.

Yoon, Hong-Key. *The Culture of Fengshui in Korea: An Exploration of East Asian Geomancy.* Lanham, MD: Lexington Books, 2006.

Yun, Sa-soon. *Critical Issues in Neo-Confucian Thought: The*

Philosophy of Yi T'oegye, translated by Michael C. Kalton. Honolulu: University of Hawaii Press, 1991.

Zhang, Qicheng. "*The Book of Changes (Yi jing)* and the Mode of Thinking of Chinese Medicine." *Contemporary Chinese Thought* 39.3 (Spring 2008): 39–58.

Zhang, Weiwen. "Religious Daoist Studies of *The Book of Changes (Yi jing)* and Their Historical and Contemporary Influence." *Contemporary Chinese Thought* 39.3 (Spring 2008): 74–97.

Zheng, Wan'geng. "Process Thinking in *The Book of Changes (Yi jing)*." *Contemporary Chinese Thought* 39.3 (Spring 2008): 59–73.

Index

As indicated in my "Preliminary Remarks," I have provided transliterations for certain non-standardized Chinese, Korean, Japanese, Vietnamese and Tibetan terms and titles in parentheses following their English translations in order to facilitate further investigations and comparisons. This approach is necessary for two reasons: (1) there are often several different translations of even the most common East Asian terms and titles; and (2) the single most important English-language reference work on the *Changes*, Bent Nielsen's *A Companion to Yi jing Numerology and Cosmology*, is organized alphabetically by Pinyin transliterations only; it has no other index. For ease of reference I have created a few special entries under which related items are grouped together and listed alphabetically under a single heading rather than scattered throughout the index—for example, the categories "trigram references" and "hexagram references." Finally, with the exception of a few particularly prominent individuals, I have not included the names of the many Westerners who have used and/or translated the *Changes*; they can be found easily enough by consulting the subsection of the main entry "*Classic of Changes (Yijing)*" under the titles "travels to the West of" and "translations of."

Cheng Yi, 93, 102–4, 148, 154, 155, 168, 230n25, 235n52

Cheng-Zhu school, 103, 107, 114, 131, 136, 142, 146, 151, 152, 153, 154, 155, 190. *See also* neo-Confucianism; orthodoxy; principle (*li*)

Chong Yagyong, 148, 149, 158

Christianity, 3, 10, 17, 18, 108, 127, 171, 172, 173, 177, 179, 180, 181, 184, 185, 190, 192, 242n56, 244n12. *See also* Jesuits

classical Chinese language, 9, 53, 129, 131, 150, 151, 156, 157, 160, 170

Classic of Changes (*Yijing*): complexity of, 12, 17, 62, 71, 86, 87, 97, 102; countercultural uses of, 10, 195–98; cultural significance of, 1, 9, 11, 13, 38, 51, 56, 74, 127, 137–39, 141, 151–52, 194–209 passim, 211, 212–23 passim (*see also* individual entries under art, literature, medicine, music, science); derivative versions of, 84, 136–37, 147, 149–150, 167, 215; globalization of, 9–11, 127–210 passim (*see also* individual entries under Japan, Korea, Vietnam and Tibet); as a mir-

ror, 62, 75, 85; as a model of the cosmos, 3, 20, 34, 60–65 passim; strategies and techniques of interpretation, xxi, 4, 5, 6, 12, 16, 17, 19, 29–30, 40–41, 68, 71, 72–74, 75–123 passim, 136, 142, 146–66 passim, 186–210 passim; translations of, xx–xxi, 12–13, 31, 127–28, 170, 180–94; travels to the West of, 171, 177, 179, 194–210. *See also* basic text; charts and diagrams; commentaries; cosmology, hexagram references; hexagram relationships; hexagrams, images; language; line statements; symbolism; Ten Wings; trigram relationships; trigrams, *Zhou Changes*

Classic of Great Mystery (*Taixuan jing*), 147, 150, 167, 215

Classic of Poetry (*Shijing*), 101–2, 154

classics, xxi, 2, 5, 11, 13, 18, 44, 45, 74, 76, 77, 93, 105, 107, 151, 154, 155, 160, 171, 172, 181, 211–12, 214; definitions of, 17, 211–12

commentaries, xxi, 1, 5, 7, 8, 21, 23, 29, 31, 32, 45–47, 48, 58,